THE NEW FOLGER LIBRARY SHAKESPEARE

Designed to make Shakespeare's great plays available to all readers, the New Folger Library edition of Shakespeare's plays provides accurate texts in modern spelling and punctuation, as well as scene-by-scene action summaries, full explanatory notes, many pictures clarifying Shakespeare's language, and notes recording all significant departures from the early printed versions. Each play is prefaced by a brief introduction, by a guide to reading Shakespeare's language, and by accounts of his life and theater. Each play is followed by an annotated list of further readings and by a "Modern Perspective" written by an expert on that particular play.

Barbara A. Mowat is Director of Academic Programs at the Folger Shakespeare Library, Executive Editor of *Shakespeare Quarterly*, Chair of the Folger Institute, and author of *The Dramaturgy of Shakespeare's Romances* and of essays on Shakespeare's plays and on the editing of the plays.

Paul Werstine is Professor of English at King's University College at The University of Western Ontario, Canada. He is general editor of the New Variorum Shakespeare and author of many papers and articles on the printing and editing of Shakespeare's plays.

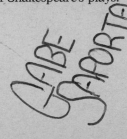

The Folger Shakespeare Library

The Folger Shakespeare Library in Washington, D.C., a privately funded research library dedicated to Shakespeare and the civilization of early modern Europe, was founded in 1932 by Henry Clay and Emily Jordan Folger. In addition to its role as the world's preeminent Shakespeare collection and its emergence as a leading center for Renaissance studies, the Folger Library offers a wide array of cultural and educational programs and services for the general public.

EDITORS

BARBARA A. MOWAT
Director of Academic Programs
Folger Shakespeare Library

PAUL WERSTINE
Professor of English
King's University College at The University of
Western Ontario, Canada

FOLGER SHAKESPEARE LIBRARY

The Merchant of Venice

By
WILLIAM SHAKESPEARE

EDITED BY BARBARA A. MOWAT
AND PAUL WERSTINE

SIMON & SCHUSTER PAPERBACKS
NEW YORK LONDON TORONTO SYDNEY

Simon & Schuster Paperbacks
A Division of Simon & Schuster, Inc.
1230 Avenue of the Americas
New York, NY 10020

Copyright © 1992 by The Folger Shakespeare Library

Washington Square Press New Folger Edition August 1992
This Simon & Schuster paperback edition August 2009

SIMON & SCHUSTER PAPERBACKS and colophon are registered trademarks of Simon & Schuster, Inc.

For information regarding special discounts for bulk purchases, please contact Simon & Schuster Special Sales at 1-866-506-1949 or business@simonandschuster.com.

The Simon & Schuster Speakers Bureau can bring authors to your live event. For more information or to book an event, contact the Simon & Schuster Speakers Bureau at 1-866-248-3049 or visit our website at www.simonspeakers.com.

Manufactured in the United States of America

25 24 23 22 21 20 19 18 17 16 15

ISBN 978-0-7434-7756-7

From the Director of the Library

For over four decades, the Folger Library General Reader's Shakespeare provided accurate and accessible texts of the plays and poems to students, teachers, and millions of other interested readers. Today, in an age often impatient with the past, the passion for Shakespeare continues to grow. No author speaks more powerfully to the human condition, in all its variety, than this actor/playwright from a minor sixteenth-century English village.

Over the years vast changes have occurred in the way Shakespeare's works are edited, performed, studied, and taught. The New Folger Library Shakespeare replaces the earlier versions, bringing to bear the best and most current thinking concerning both the texts and their interpretation. Here is an edition which makes the plays and poems fully understandable for modern readers using uncompromising scholarship. Professors Barbara Mowat and Paul Werstine are uniquely qualified to produce this New Folger Shakespeare for a new generation of readers. The Library is grateful for the learning, clarity, and imagination they have brought to this ambitious project.

Werner Gundersheimer,
Director of the Folger Shakespeare
Library from 1984 to 2002

Contents

Editors' Preface   ix
Shakespeare's *The Merchant of Venice*   xiii
Reading Shakespeare's Language:
  The Merchant of Venice   xiv
Shakespeare's Life   xxiv
Shakespeare's Theater   xxxii
The Publication of Shakespeare's Plays   xli
An Introduction to This Text   xlv

The Merchant of Venice
  Text of the Play with Commentary   1

Textual Notes   205
The Merchant of Venice: A Modern Perspective
  by Alexander Leggatt   211
Further Reading   221
Key to Famous Lines and Phrases   235

Editors' Preface

In recent years, ways of dealing with Shakespeare's texts and with the interpretation of his plays have been undergoing significant change. This edition, while retaining many of the features that have always made the Folger Shakespeare so attractive to the general reader, at the same time reflects these current ways of thinking about Shakespeare. For example, modern readers, actors, and teachers have become interested in the differences between, on the one hand, the early forms in which Shakespeare's plays were first published and, on the other hand, the forms in which editors through the centuries have presented them. In response to this interest, we have based our edition on what we consider the best early printed version of a particular play (explaining our rationale in a section called "An Introduction to This Text") and have marked our changes in the text—unobtrusively, we hope, but in such a way that the curious reader can be aware that a change has been made and can consult the "Textual Notes" to discover what appeared in the early printed version.

Current ways of looking at the plays are reflected in our brief introductions, in many of the commentary notes, in the annotated lists of "Further Reading," and especially in each play's "Modern Perspective," an essay written by an outstanding scholar who brings to the reader his or her fresh assessment of the play in the light of today's interests and concerns.

As in the Folger Library General Reader's Shakespeare, which this edition replaces, we include explanatory notes designed to help make Shakespeare's language clearer to a modern reader, and we place the notes on the page facing the text that they explain. We also follow the earlier edition in including illustrations —of objects, of clothing, of mythological figures—from books and manuscripts in the Folger Library collection. We provide fresh accounts of the life of Shakespeare, of the publishing of his plays, and of the theaters in which his plays were performed, as well as an introduction to the text itself. We also include a section called "Reading Shakespeare's Language," in which we try to help readers learn to "break the code" of Elizabethan poetic language.

For each section of each volume, we are indebted to a host of generous experts and fellow scholars. The "Reading Shakespeare's Language" sections, for example, could not have been written had not Arthur King, of Brigham Young University, and Randal Robinson, author of *Unlocking Shakespeare's Language*, led the way in untangling Shakespearean language puzzles and shared their insights and methodologies generously with us. "Shakespeare's Life" profited by the careful reading given it by S. Schoenbaum, "Shakespeare's Theater" was read and strengthened by Andrew Gurr and John Astington, and "The Publication of Shakespeare's Plays" is indebted to the comments of Peter W. M. Blayney. We, as editors, take sole responsibility for any errors in our editions.

We are grateful to the authors of the "Modern Perspectives," to Leeds Barroll and David Bevington for their generous encouragement, to the Huntington and Newberry Libraries for fellowship support, to King's College for the grants it has provided to Paul Werstine, to the Social Sciences and Humanities Research Council of Canada, which provided him with a Research Time Stipend for 1990–91, and to the Folger Institute's Center for Shakespeare Studies for its fortuitous sponsorship of a workshop on "Shakespeare's Texts for Students and Teachers" (funded by the National Endowment for the

Humanities and led by Richard Knowles of the University of Wisconsin), a workshop from which we learned an enormous amount about what is wanted by college and high-school teachers of Shakespeare today.

Our biggest debt is to the Folger Shakespeare Library: to Werner Gundersheimer, Director of the Library, who has made possible our edition; to Jean Miller, the Library's Art Curator, who combed the Library holdings for illustrations, and to Julie Ainsworth, Head of the Photography Department, who carefully photographed them; to Peggy O'Brien, Director of Education, who gave us expert advice about the needs being expressed by Shakespeare teachers and students (and to Martha Christian and other "master teachers" who used our texts in manuscript in their classrooms); to the staff of the Academic Programs Division, especially Paul Menzer (who drafted "Further Reading" material), Mary Tonkinson, Lena Cowen Orlin, Molly Haws, and Jessica Hymowitz; and, finally, to the staff of the Library Reading Room, whose patience and support have been invaluable.

Barbara A. Mowat and Paul Werstine

Venice.
From Giacomo Franco, *Habiti d'huomeni . . .* (1609?).

Shakespeare's
The Merchant of Venice

The Merchant of Venice, like most of Shakespeare's comedies, is about love and marriage. But the path to marriage in this play is unusually hazardous. The characters compare it to the epic voyage undertaken by Jason and the Argonauts to win the Golden Fleece. In this play, Portia, the fabulously wealthy heiress of Belmont, is herself the Golden Fleece, according to her would-be husband, Bassanio. To win her hand in marriage, he must put his future at risk in an attempt to choose correctly among three caskets or chests of gold, silver, and lead. If he chooses rightly, he wins, in marriage, the beautiful, intelligent, and supremely resourceful Portia and her great wealth. If he chooses wrongly, he must forever abandon Portia and may never propose marriage to any other woman. He would therefore die without legal heirs.

And the test of the caskets, prescribed in the will of Portia's dead father, is not the only obstacle to Bassanio and Portia's happiness. There also stands against them a magnificent villain, the moneylender Shylock. In creating this character, Shakespeare seems to have shared in a widespread and, from our point of view, despicable prejudice against Jews. In Shakespeare's England there had been no Jews for a long time, except an occasional visitor, and so there was no direct experience to counteract the prejudice. Shylock would have been regarded as a villain simply because he was a Jew. Yet Shakespeare was led by his art of language to put onstage a character who gave such powerful expression to the alienation he felt because of the hatred around him that, in many productions of the play and in the opinions of many famous actors, Shylock emerges the hero of *The Merchant of Venice*. In fashioning in Shylock a character whose function is to frustrate the satisfaction that we are invited to desire for the play's lovers, Shakespeare has, for many people, brought forth a character who rivals the lovers in the power he exerts over us.

Over the centuries Portia too has deeply engaged audiences. In her role as the daughter bound by her father's will, one who sees herself as helpless in the face of the casket test and whose anxieties and joys we are encouraged to share, Portia is, for readers and playgoers alike, one of Shakespeare's most appealing heroines. But it is in her role as Balthazar the young lawyer that Portia is most remembered. The speech in which she urges Shylock to show the kind of mercy that "droppeth as the gentle rain from heaven," that "is enthronèd in the hearts of kings" and "is an attribute to God Himself," is one of Shakespeare's most famous and most loved passages. For readers and audiences today, the pleasure that should accompany her saving of Antonio is clouded by what seems to us her cruel treatment of Shylock—but the role of Portia remains one that every Shakespearean actress yearns to play.

After you have read the play, we invite you to turn to the back of this book and read *"The Merchant of Venice: A Modern Perspective"* by Professor Alexander Leggatt of the University of Toronto.

Reading Shakespeare's Language

For many people today, reading Shakespeare's language can be a problem—but it is a problem that can be solved. Those who have studied Latin (or even French or

German or Spanish) and those who are used to reading poetry will have little difficulty in understanding the language of Shakespeare's poetic drama. Others, however, need to develop the skills of untangling unusual sentence structures and of recognizing and understanding poetic compressions, omissions, and wordplay. And even those skilled in reading unusual sentence structures may have occasional trouble with Shakespeare's words. Four hundred years of "static"—caused by changes in language and in life—intervene between his speaking and our hearing. Most of his immense vocabulary is still in use, but a few of his words are not, and, worse, some of his words now have meanings quite different from those they had in the sixteenth century. In the theater, most of these difficulties are solved for us by actors who study the language and articulate it for us so that the essential meaning is heard—or, when combined with stage action, is at least *felt*. When reading on one's own, one must do what each actor does: go over the lines (often with a dictionary close at hand) until the puzzles are solved and the lines yield up their poetry and the characters speak in words and phrases that are, suddenly, rewarding and wonderfully memorable.

Shakespeare's Words

As you begin to read the opening scenes of a play by Shakespeare, you may notice occasional unfamiliar words. Some are unfamiliar simply because we no longer use them. In the opening scenes of *The Merchant of Venice*, for example, we find the words *sooth* (i.e., truth), *piring* (i.e., peering), *an* (i.e., if), and *doit* (i.e., jot). Words of this kind are explained in notes to the text and will become familiar the more of Shakespeare's plays you read.

Some words are strange not because of the "static" introduced by changes in language over the past centuries but because these are words that Shakespeare is using to build a dramatic world that has its own geography and history and story. *The Merchant of Venice* is an interesting example of the way Shakespeare uses words to build dramatic worlds, for in this play he must build two such worlds—the mercantile world of Venice and the romantic world of Portia's estate of Belmont. In the first and third scenes of the play, he builds—through references to "argosies," to "signiors," to "ventures," to "shallows," to "ducats," to "the Rialto," to "usances" —a Venetian location inhabited by moneylenders and merchants who venture their fortunes at sea; in the same scenes, he builds a background mythology that underlies Bassanio's quest, referring to "Jason," to the "Golden Fleece," and to "Colchos' strond." In the second and fourth scenes, where he shifts us to Belmont and to the test that Portia's suitors must undergo, he includes, within the discussions of Portia's father's will and the "lott'ry of [Portia's] destiny," references to "caskets" (i.e., small ornamental chests for holding jewels and other valuables), to "the Sophy" and to "Sultan Solyman," and builds another background mythology through references to "Sibylla" and "Diana," to "Phoebus," and to "Alcides." These "local" references (each of which will be explained in notes to this text) create the worlds that Antonio, Bassanio, and Shylock inhabit in Venice and that Portia and Nerissa inhabit at Belmont, worlds (and references) that will become increasingly familiar to you as you get further into the play.

In *The Merchant of Venice*, as in all of Shakespeare's writing, the most problematic words are those that we still use but that we use with a different meaning. In the opening scenes of *The Merchant of Venice*, we find the word *still* where we would use "always," the word *straight* where we would say "at once" or "immediately," the word *disabled* where we would use "depleted" or "reduced," the word *ripe* where we would say "urgent." Again, such words will be explained in the notes to this text, but they, too, will become familiar as you continue to read Shakespeare's language.

Shakespeare's Sentences

In an English sentence, meaning is quite dependent on the place given each word. "The dog bit the boy" and "The boy bit the dog" mean very different things, even though the individual words are the same. Because English places such importance on the positions of words in sentences, on the way words are arranged, unusual arrangements can puzzle a reader. Shakespeare frequently shifts his sentences away from "normal" English arrangements—often in order to create the rhythm he seeks, sometimes in order to use a line's poetic rhythm to emphasize a particular word, sometimes to give a character his or her own speech patterns or to allow the character to speak in a special way. Again, when we attend a good performance of the play, the actors will have worked out the sentence structures and will articulate the sentences so that the meaning is clear. In reading for yourself, do as the actor does. That is, when you become puzzled by a character's speech, check to see if words are being presented in an unusual sequence.

Look first for the placement of subject and verb. Shakespeare often rearranges verbs and subjects (e.g., instead of "He goes," we find "Goes he," or instead of "He does not go," we find "He goes not"). In the opening line of *The Merchant of Venice*, when Antonio says *"I know not* why I am so sad,'' he is using such a construction; Salarino does so as well when, at 1.1.40, he says "But tell not me,'' as does Antonio again at 1.1.46, "Therefore my merchandise makes me not sad.'' Such inversions, which occur frequently in *The Merchant of Venice*, rarely cause much confusion. More problematic are Shakespeare's placings of the object or the predicate adjective before the subject and verb (e.g., instead of "I hit him,'' we might find "Him I hit,'' or instead of "It is white,'' we might find "White it is''). Though frequent in many of Shakespeare's plays, such inversions are rare in *The Merchant of Venice*. One does find, at 1.1.191, Antonio saying "I no question make,'' and, at 2.4.14–15, Lorenzo saying "whiter than the paper it writ on / Is the fair hand that writ'' (where the normal arrangement would be "the fair hand is whiter . . .'') and, at 2.7.64–65, Morocco saying "But here an angel in a golden bed / Lies all within'' (where one would normally say "an angel lies here . . .''). The language of this play, though, is unusual in its avoidance of this kind of inversion.

Inversions are not the only unusual sentence structures in Shakespeare's language. Often his sentences separate words that would normally appear together. (This is often done to create a particular rhythm or to stress a particular word.) In Antonio's lines at 1.1.143–44, "And if it stand, as you yourself still do, / Within the eye of honor,'' the clause "as you yourself still do'' interrupts the normal construction "stand within''; in Shylock's lines at 1.3.48–50, "he rails, / Even there where merchants most do congregate, / On me, my bargains, and my well-won thrift,'' the line "Even there where merchants most do congregate'' interrupts the construction "rails on.'' Bassanio, at 1.1.153–54, says "I owe you much, and, *like a willful youth,* / That which I owe is lost,'' and at 1.1.169–70 says "she is fair, and, *fairer than that word,* / Of wondrous virtues." In both these sentences, he separates "and" from the words that would normally follow. In order to create for yourself sentences that seem more like the English of everyday speech, you may wish to rearrange the words, putting together the word clusters ("stand within the eye of honor," "rails on me," "and that which I owe is lost"), placing the remaining words in their more familiar order. You will usually find that the sentence will gain in clarity but will lose its rhythm or shift its emphasis. You can then see for yourself why Shakespeare chose his own unusual arrangement.

Locating and rearranging words that "belong together" is especially necessary in passages that separate subjects from verbs and verbs from objects by long delaying or expanding interruptions. We find such a passage at 1.1.9–12, when Salarino says,

> There where your *argosies* with portly sail
> (Like signiors and rich burghers on the flood,
> Or, as it were, the pageants of the sea)
> *Do overpeer* the petty traffickers. . . .

Here, the subject "argosies" is widely separated from the verb "do overpeer." In plays written some years later than *The Merchant of Venice* (in *Hamlet,* for example), long interrupted constructions are used frequently and for complicated dramatic purposes. They are relatively rare in *The Merchant of Venice.*

Shakespeare's sentences are sometimes complicated not because of unusual structures or interruptions but because he omits words and parts of words that English sentences normally require. (In conversation, we, too, often omit words. We say, "Heard from him yet?" and our hearer supplies the missing "Have you." Frequent reading of Shakespeare—and of other poets—trains us to supply such missing words.) When Gratiano says, at 1.1.114–16, "Well, keep me company but two years more, / Thou shalt not know the sound of thine own tongue," he omits the words "if you" before "keep." Bassanio, at line 1.1.168, omits the word "there" in saying "In Belmont [there] is a lady richly left." As with interrupted constructions, in plays written some years after *The Merchant of Venice* Shakespeare uses omissions both of verbs and of nouns to great dramatic effect. In *The Merchant of Venice* omissions are few and seem to be used primarily to create regular iambic pentameter lines.

Finally, one finds in all of Shakespeare's plays constructions that do not fit any particular category and that must be untangled on their own. In *The Merchant of Venice* 1.1.85, for example, one finds "old wrinkles," meaning "the wrinkles of old age." (One finds a comparable construction in *Julius Caesar* 1.2.11, where "sterile curse" means "curse of sterility.") Again, in *The Merchant of Venice* one finds "melancholy bait" (1.1.107), which is to be understood to mean "the bait of melancholy." Such constructions are explained in the notes to this text, and must simply be handled as individual puzzles to be solved.

Shakespearean Wordplay

Shakespeare plays with language so often and so variously that entire books are written on the topic. Here we will mention only four of the ways he plays with language—puns, malapropisms, metaphors, and similes. A pun is a play on words that sound the same but that have different meanings. When, in the third scene of *The Merchant of Venice*, Shylock says "suff'rance is the badge of all our tribe" (line 120), he seems to be playing on two

meanings of *sufferance* ("forbearance" and "suffering");
his line "And all for use of that which is mine own" (line
123) contains a pun on the word *use*, which means both
"lending with interest" and "putting to use." The pun
that is heard most often in this play is that on *gentle/
gentile*. It is not always clear when we are to hear
"gentle" as "gentile," but in several cases—e.g., "gentle
Jew" (1.3.190), "If e'er the Jew her father come to
heaven, / It will be for his gentle daughter's sake"
(2.4.37–38), "Now, by my hood, a gentle and no Jew!"
(2.6.53), and "We all expect a gentle answer, Jew"
(4.1.35)—it seems likely that the pun is intended.

In many of Shakespeare's plays, puns are used frequently, either for comic effect (as in *Taming of the
Shrew*) or for a wide variety of effects (as in *Romeo and
Juliet*). In *The Merchant of Venice*, as the above examples
show, they are used rather seriously. In the play's more
comic scenes, one finds, instead of puns, words that are
called "malapropisms"—i.e., words grotesquely mis-
used. Lancelet Gobbo and his father, Old Gobbo, are
both given to malapropisms. In 2.2, for example, Lancelet uses *incarnation* for "incarnate" and *impertinent* for
"pertinent"; Old Gobbo uses *infection* for "affection"
and *defect* for "effect." In 2.5, Lancelet uses *reproach* for
"approach," and, in 3.5., *agitation* for "cogitation."

A metaphor is a play on words in which one object or
idea is expressed as if it were something else, something
with which it shares common features. For instance,
when Bassanio says to Antonio (1.1.154–58) "if you
please / To shoot another arrow that self way / Which
you did shoot the first, I do not doubt, / As I will watch
the aim, or to find both / Or bring your latter hazard
back again," he uses metaphoric language in which
Antonio's loan of money to Bassanio is represented as
an arrow: Antonio is encouraged to shoot a second
arrow in the same direction as he shot the first and thus

recover both of them (i.e., get back both the loan that Bassanio is now asking for, as well as the first loan, now lost).

Metaphors are often used when the idea being conveyed is hard to express, and the speaker is thus given language that helps to carry the idea or the feeling to his or her listener—and to the audience. In many of Shakespeare's plays, metaphors play a central role in expressing characters' feeling. In *The Merchant of Venice,* one is more likely to find similes—comparisons between two entities that are expressed by saying that one is *like* or *as* the other. When Bassanio describes Portia to Antonio, for instance, he says that "her sunny locks / Hang on her temples like a golden fleece, / Which makes her seat of Belmont Colchos' strond, / And many Jasons come in quest of her" (1.1.176–79), thus equating her hair to the Golden Fleece, her estate of Belmont to the land where the Fleece was to be found, and her suitors to Jason. When Portia stands apart as Bassanio makes his choice of the caskets, she explains her feelings in an elaborate series of similes that begins as follows: "Let music sound while he doth make his choice. / Then if he lose he makes a swanlike end, / Fading in music. That the comparison / May stand more proper, my eye shall be the stream / And wat'ry deathbed for him" (3.2.45–49). And when Portia explains about "the quality of mercy," she uses a simile to convey the way that this quality operates: "It droppeth as the gentle rain from heaven / Upon the place beneath" (4.1.191–92).

Implied Stage Action

Finally, in reading Shakespeare's plays you should always remember that what you are reading is a performance script. The dialogue is written to be spoken by actors who, at the same time, are moving, gesturing, picking up objects, weeping, shaking their fists. Some stage action is described in what are called "stage directions"; some is suggested within the dialogue itself. Learn to be alert to such signals as you stage the play in your imagination. When, in 2.6 of *The Merchant of Venice*, Jessica says "Here, catch this casket; it is worth the pains," it is clear that she throws a chest of jewels and money from her window. When, in the trial scene (4.1) Bassanio says "Why dost thou whet thy knife so earnestly?" it is clear, from Gratiano's later line, "Not on thy sole but on thy soul, harsh Jew," that Shylock sharpens his knife on the sole of his shoe. However, many moments are much less clear. When, for instance, Shylock describes Antonio's entrance in 3.1 with the words "How like a fawning publican he looks!" it is unclear just what Antonio does that leads Shylock to say this. Nor is it clear how the scene between Lancelet and his nearly blind father should be played. We know that Lancelet kneels (his father tells him to stand up); then his father says: "Lord worshiped might He be, what a beard hast thou got! Thou hast got more hair on thy chin than Dobbin my fill-horse has on his tail." To which Lancelet responds, "It should seem, then, that Dobbin's tail grows backward. I am sure he had more hair of his tail than I have of my face when I last saw him." Stage tradition has Lancelet, when he kneels, turn his back to his father, so that the father mistakes his son's long hair for a beard—but this is a moment when the director (and you, as a reader, in your imagination) can decide just how the joke should be staged.

It is immensely rewarding to work carefully with Shakespeare's language so that the words, the sentences, the wordplay, and the implied stage action all become clear—as readers for the past four centuries have discovered. It may be more pleasurable to attend a good performance of a play—though not everyone has thought so. But the joy of being able to stage one of Shakespeare's plays in one's imagination, to return to passages that continue to yield further meanings (or further questions) the more one reads them—these are pleasures that, for many, rival (or at least augment) those of the performed text, and certainly make it worth considerable effort to "break the code" of Elizabethan poetic drama and let free the remarkable language that makes up a Shakespeare text.

Shakespeare's Life

Surviving documents that give us glimpses into the life of William Shakespeare show us a playwright, poet, and actor who grew up in the market town of Stratford-upon-Avon, spent his professional life in London, and returned to Stratford a wealthy landowner. He was born in April 1564, died in April 1616, and is buried inside the chancel of Holy Trinity Church in Stratford.

We wish we could know more about the life of the world's greatest dramatist. His plays and poems are testaments to his wide reading—especially to his knowledge of Virgil, Ovid, Plutarch, Holinshed's *Chronicles*, and the Bible—and to his mastery of the English language, but we can only speculate about his education. We know that the King's New School in Stratford-upon-Avon was considered excellent. The school was one of the English "grammar schools" established to educate young men, primarily in Latin grammar and literature. As in other schools of the time, students began their studies at the age of four or five in the attached "petty school," and there learned to read and write in English, studying primarily the catechism from the Book of Common Prayer. After two years in the petty school, students entered the lower form (grade) of the grammar school, where they began the serious study of Latin grammar and Latin texts that would occupy most of the remainder of their school days. (Several Latin texts that Shakespeare used repeatedly in writing his plays and poems were texts that schoolboys memorized and recited.) Latin comedies were introduced early in the lower form; in the upper form, which the boys entered at age ten or eleven, students wrote their own Latin orations and declamations, studied Latin historians and rhetoricians, and began the study of Greek using the Greek New Testament.

Since the records of the Stratford "grammar school" do not survive, we cannot prove that William Shakespeare attended the school; however, every indication (his father's position as an alderman and bailiff of Stratford, the playwright's own knowledge of the Latin classics, scenes in the plays that recall grammar-school experiences—for example, *The Merry Wives of Windsor*, 4.1) suggests that he did. We also lack generally accepted documentation about Shakespeare's life after his schooling ended and his professional life in London began. His marriage in 1582 (at age eighteen) to Anne Hathaway and the subsequent births of his daughter Susanna (1583) and the twins Judith and Hamnet (1585) are recorded, but how he supported himself and where he lived are not known. Nor do we know when and why he left Stratford for the London theatrical world, nor how he rose to be the important figure in that world that he had become by the early 1590s.

We do know that by 1592 he had achieved some prominence in London as both an actor and a playwright. In that year was published a book by the playwright Robert Greene attacking an actor who had the audacity to write blank-verse drama and who was "in his own conceit [i.e., opinion] the only "Shakescene in a country." Since Greene's attack includes a parody of a line from one of Shakespeare's early plays, there is little doubt that it is Shakespeare to whom he refers, a "Shake-scene" who had aroused Greene's fury by successfully competing with university-educated dramatists like Greene himself. It was in 1593 that Shakespeare became a published poet. In that year he published his long narrative poem *Venus and Adonis;* in 1594, he followed it with *The Rape of Lucrece.* Both poems were dedicated to the young earl of Southampton (Henry Wriothesley), who may have become Shakespeare's patron.

It seems no coincidence that Shakespeare wrote these narrative poems at a time when the theaters were closed because of the plague, a contagious epidemic disease that devastated the population of London. When the theaters reopened in 1594, Shakespeare apparently resumed his double career of actor and playwright and began his long (and seemingly profitable) service as an acting-company shareholder. Records for December of 1594 show him to be a leading member of the Lord Chamberlain's Men. It was this company of actors, later named the King's Men, for whom he would be a principal actor, dramatist, and shareholder for the rest of his career.

So far as we can tell, that career spanned about twenty years. In the 1590s, he wrote his plays on English history as well as several comedies and at least two tragedies (*Titus Andronicus* and *Romeo and Juliet*). These histories, comedies, and tragedies are the plays credited to him in 1598 in a work, *Palladis Tamia*, that in one chapter compares English writers with "Greek, Latin, and Italian Poets." There the author, Francis Meres, claims that Shakespeare is comparable to the Latin dramatists Seneca for tragedy and Plautus for comedy, and calls him "the most excellent in both kinds for the stage." He also names him "mellifluous and honey-tongued Shakespeare": "I say," writes Meres, "that the Muses would speak with Shakespeare's fine filed phrase, if they would speak English." Since Meres also mentions Shakespeare's "sugared sonnets among his private friends," it is assumed that many of Shakespeare's sonnets (not published until 1609) were also written in the 1590s.

In 1599, Shakespeare's company built a theater for themselves across the river from London, naming it the Globe. The plays that are considered by many to be Shakespeare's major tragedies (*Hamlet, Othello, King Lear,* and *Macbeth*) were written while the company was resident in this theater, as were such comedies as *Twelfth Night* and *Measure for Measure.* Many of Shakespeare's plays were performed at court (both for Queen Elizabeth I and, after her death in 1603, for King James I), some were presented at the Inns of Court (the residences of London's legal societies), and some were doubtless performed in other towns, at the universities, and at great houses when the King's Men went on tour; otherwise, his plays from 1599 to 1608 were, so far as we know, performed only at the Globe. Between 1608 and 1612, Shakespeare wrote several plays—among them *The Winter's Tale* and *The Tempest*—presumably for the company's new indoor Blackfriars theater, though the plays seem to have been performed also at the Globe and at court. Surviving documents describe a performance of *The Winter's Tale* in 1611 at the Globe, for example, and performances of *The Tempest* in 1611 and 1613 at the royal palace of Whitehall.

Shakespeare wrote very little after 1612, the year in which he probably wrote *King Henry VIII.* (It was at a performance of *Henry VIII* in 1613 that the Globe caught fire and burned to the ground.) Sometime between 1610 and 1613 he seems to have returned to live in Stratford-upon-Avon, where he owned a large house and considerable property, and where his wife and his two daughters and their husbands lived. (His son Hamnet had died in 1596.) During his professional years in London, Shakespeare had presumably derived income from the acting company's profits as well as from his own career as an actor, from the sale of his play manuscripts to the acting company, and, after 1599, from his shares as an owner of the Globe. It was presumably that income, carefully invested in land and other property, that made him the wealthy man that surviving documents show him to have become. It is also assumed that William Shakespeare's growing wealth and reputation played some part in inclining the crown, in 1596, to grant John Shakespeare, William's father, the coat of arms that he had so long sought. William Shakespeare died in Stratford on April 23, 1616 (according to the epitaph carved under his bust in Holy Trinity Church) and was buried on April 25. Seven years after his death, his collected plays were published as *Mr. William Shakespeares Comedies, Histories, & Tragedies* (the work now known as the First Folio).

The years in which Shakespeare wrote were among the most exciting in English history. Intellectually, the discovery, translation, and printing of Greek and Roman classics were making available a set of works and worldviews that interacted complexly with Christian texts and beliefs. The result was a questioning, a vital intellectual ferment, that provided energy for the period's amazing dramatic and literary output and that fed directly into Shakespeare's plays. The Ghost in *Hamlet*, for example, is wonderfully complicated in part because he is a figure from Roman tragedy—the spirit of the dead returning to seek revenge—who at the same time inhabits a Christian hell (or purgatory); Hamlet's description of humankind reflects at one moment the Neoplatonic wonderment at mankind ("What a piece of work is a man!") and, at the next, the Christian disparagement of human sinners ("And yet, to me, what is this quintessence of dust?").

As intellectual horizons expanded, so also did geographical and cosmological horizons. New worlds—both North and South America—were explored, and in them were found human beings who lived and worshiped in ways radically different from those of Renaissance Europeans and Englishmen. The universe during these years also seemed to shift and expand. Copernicus had earlier theorized that the earth was not the center of the cosmos but revolved as a planet around the sun. Galileo's telescope, created in 1609, allowed scientists to see that Copernicus had been correct: the universe was not organized with the earth at the center, nor was it so nicely circumscribed as people had, until that time, thought. In terms of expanding horizons, the impact of these discoveries on people's beliefs—religious, scientific, and philosophical—cannot be overstated.

London, too, rapidly expanded and changed during the years (from the early 1590s to around 1610) that Shakespeare lived there. London—the center of England's government, its economy, its royal court, its overseas trade—was, during these years, becoming an exciting metropolis, drawing to it thousands of new citizens every year. Troubled by overcrowding, by poverty, by recurring epidemics of the plague, London was also a mecca for the wealthy and the aristocratic, and for those who sought advancement at court, or power in government or finance or trade. One hears in Shakespeare's plays the voices of London—the struggles for power, the fear of venereal disease, the language of buying and selling. One hears as well the voices of Stratford-upon-Avon—references to the nearby Forest of Arden, to sheep herding, to small-town gossip, to village fairs and markets. Part of the richness of Shakespeare's work is the influence felt there of the various worlds in which he lived: the world of metropolitan London, the world of small-town and rural England, the world of the theater, and the worlds of craftsmen and shepherds.

That Shakespeare inhabited such worlds we know from surviving London and Stratford documents, as well as from the evidence of the plays and poems themselves. From such records we can sketch the dramatist's life. We know from his works that he was a voracious reader. We know from legal and business documents that he was a multifaceted theater man who became a wealthy landowner. We know a bit about his family life and a fair amount about his legal and financial dealings. Most scholars today depend upon such evidence as they draw their picture of the world's greatest playwright. Such, however, has not always been the case. Until the late eighteenth century, the William Shakespeare who lived in most biographies was the creation of legend and tradition. This was the Shakespeare who was supposedly caught poaching deer at Charlecote, the estate of Sir Thomas Lucy close by Stratford; this was the Shakespeare who fled from Sir Thomas's vengeance and made his way in London by taking care of horses outside a playhouse; this was the Shakespeare who reportedly could barely read, but whose natural gifts were extraordinary, whose father was a butcher who allowed his gifted son sometimes to help in the butcher shop, where William supposedly killed calves "in a high style," making a speech for the occasion. It was this legendary William Shakespeare whose Falstaff (in *1* and *2 Henry IV*) so pleased Queen Elizabeth that she demanded a play about Falstaff in love, and demanded that it be written in fourteen days (hence the existence of *The Merry Wives of Windsor*). It was this legendary Shakespeare who reached the top of his acting career in the roles of the Ghost in *Hamlet* and old Adam in *As You Like It*—and who died of a fever contracted by drinking too hard at "a merry meeting" with the poets Michael Drayton and Ben Jonson. This legendary Shakespeare is a rambunctious, undisciplined man, as attractively "wild" as his plays were seen by earlier generations to be. Unfortunately, there is no trace of evidence to support these wonderful stories.

Perhaps in response to the disreputable Shakespeare of legend—or perhaps in response to the fragmentary and, for some, all-too-ordinary Shakespeare documented by surviving records—some people since the mid-nineteenth century have argued that William Shakespeare could not have written the plays that bear his name. These persons have put forward some dozen names as more likely authors, among them Queen Elizabeth, Sir Francis Bacon, Edward de Vere (earl of Oxford), and Christopher Marlowe. Such attempts to find what for these people is a more believable author of the plays is a tribute to the regard in which the plays are held. Unfortunately for their claims, the documents that exist that provide evidence for the facts of Shakespeare's life tie him inextricably to the body of plays and poems that bear his name. Unlikely as it seems to those who want the works to have been written by an aristocrat, a university graduate, or an "important" person, the plays and poems seem clearly to have been produced by a man from Stratford-upon-Avon with a very good "grammar-school" education and a life of experience in London and in the world of the London theater. How this particular man produced the works that dominate the cultures of much of the world almost four hundred years after his death is one of life's mysteries—and one that will continue to tease our imaginations as we continue to delight in his plays and poems.

Shakespeare's Theater

The actors of Shakespeare's time are known to have performed plays in a great variety of locations. They played at court (that is, in the great halls of such royal residences as Whitehall, Hampton Court, and Greenwich); they played in halls at the universities of Oxford and Cambridge, and at the Inns of Court (the residences in London of the legal societies); and they also played in the private houses of great lords and civic officials. Sometimes acting companies went on tour from London into the provinces, often (but not only) when outbreaks of bubonic plague in the capital forced the closing of theaters to reduce the possibility of contagion in crowded audiences. In the provinces the actors usually staged their plays in churches (until around 1600) or in guildhalls. While surviving records show only a handful of occasions when actors played at inns while on tour, London inns were important playing places up until the 1590s.

The building of theaters in London had begun only shortly before Shakespeare wrote his first plays in the 1590s. These theaters were of two kinds: outdoor or public playhouses that could accommodate large numbers of playgoers, and indoor or private theaters for much smaller audiences. What is usually regarded as the first London outdoor public playhouse was called simply the Theatre. James Burbage—the father of Richard Burbage, who was perhaps the most famous actor in Shakespeare's company—built it in 1576 in an area north of the city of London called Shoreditch. Among the more famous of the other public playhouses that capitalized on the new fashion were the Curtain and the Fortune (both also built north of the city), the Rose, the Swan, the Globe, and the Hope (all located on the Bankside, a region just across the Thames south of the city of London). All these playhouses had to be built outside the jurisdiction of the city of London because many civic officials were hostile to the performance of drama and repeatedly petitioned the royal council to abolish it.

The theaters erected on the Bankside (a region under the authority of the Church of England, whose head was the monarch) shared the neighborhood with houses of prostitution and with the Paris Garden, where the blood sports of bearbaiting and bullbaiting were carried on. There may have been no clear distinction between playhouses and buildings for such sports, for we know that the Hope was used for both plays and baiting and that Philip Henslowe, owner of the Rose and, later, partner in the ownership of the Fortune, was also a partner in a monopoly on baiting. All these forms of entertainment were easily accessible to Londoners by boat across the Thames or over London Bridge.

Evidently Shakespeare's company prospered on the Bankside. They moved there in 1599. Threatened by difficulties in renewing the lease on the land where their first theater (the Theatre) had been built, Shakespeare's company took advantage of the Christmas holiday in 1598 to dismantle the Theatre and transport its timbers across the Thames to the Bankside, where, in 1599, these timbers were used in the building of the Globe. The weather in late December 1598 is recorded as having been especially harsh. It was so cold that the

Thames was "nigh [nearly] frozen," and there was heavy snow. Perhaps the weather aided Shakespeare's company in eluding their landlord, the snow hiding their activity and the freezing of the Thames allowing them to slide the timbers across to the Bankside without paying tolls for repeated trips over London Bridge. Attractive as this narrative is, it remains just as likely that the heavy snow hampered transport of the timbers in wagons through the London streets to the river. It also must be remembered that the Thames was, according to report, only "nigh frozen" and therefore as impassable as it ever was. Whatever the precise circumstances of this fascinating event in English theater history, Shakespeare's company was able to begin playing at their new Globe theater on the Bankside in 1599. After the first Globe burned down in 1613 during the staging of Shakespeare's *Henry VIII* (its thatch roof was set alight by cannon fire called for by the performance), Shakespeare's company immediately rebuilt on the same location. The second Globe seems to have been a grander structure than its predecessor. It remained in use until the beginning of the English Civil War in 1642, when Parliament officially closed the theaters. Soon thereafter it was pulled down.

The public theaters of Shakespeare's time were very different buildings from our theaters today. First of all, they were open-air playhouses. As recent excavations of the Rose and the Globe confirm, some were polygonal or roughly circular in shape; the Fortune, however, was square. The most recent estimates of their size put the diameter of these buildings at 72 feet (the Rose) to 100 feet (the Globe), but we know that they held vast audiences of two or three thousand, who must have been squeezed together quite tightly. Some of these spectators paid extra to sit or stand in the two or three levels of roofed galleries that extended, on the upper levels, all the way around the theater and surrounded an open space. In this space were the stage and, perhaps, the tiring house (what we would call dressing rooms), as well as the so-called yard. In the yard stood the spectators who chose to pay less, the ones whom Hamlet contemptuously called "groundlings." For a roof they had only the sky, and so they were exposed to all kinds of weather. They stood on a floor that was sometimes made of mortar and sometimes of ash mixed with the shells of hazelnuts. The latter provided a porous and therefore dry footing for the crowd, and the shells may have been more comfortable to stand on because they were not as hard as mortar. Availability of shells may not have been a problem if hazelnuts were a favorite food for Shakespeare's audiences to munch on as they watched his plays. Archaeologists who are today unearthing the remains of theaters from this period have discovered quantities of these nutshells on theater sites.

Unlike the yard, the stage itself was covered by a roof. Its ceiling, called "the heavens," is thought to have been elaborately painted to depict the sun, moon, stars, and planets. Just how big the stage was remains hard to determine. We have a single sketch of part of the interior of the Swan. A Dutchman named Johannes de Witt visited this theater around 1596 and sent a sketch of it back to his friend, Arend van Buchel. Because van Buchel found de Witt's letter and sketch of interest, he copied both into a book. It is van Buchel's copy, adapted, it seems, to the shape and size of the page in his book, that survives. In this sketch, the stage appears to be a large rectangular platform that thrusts far out into the yard, perhaps even as far as the center of the circle formed by the surrounding galleries. This drawing, combined with the specifications for the size of the stage in the building contract for the Fortune, has led scholars to conjecture that the stage on which Shakespeare's plays were performed must have measured approximately 43 feet in width and 27 feet in depth, a vast acting area. But the digging up of a large part of the Rose by archaeologists has provided evidence of a quite different stage design. The Rose stage was a platform tapered at the corners and much shallower than what seems to be depicted in the van Buchel sketch. Indeed, its measurements seem to be about 37.5 feet across at its widest point and only 15.5 feet deep. Because the surviving indications of stage size and design differ from each other so much, it is possible that the stages in other theaters, like the Theatre, the Curtain, and the Globe (the outdoor playhouses where we know that Shakespeare's plays were performed), were different from those at both the Swan and the Rose.

After about 1608 Shakespeare's plays were staged not only at the Globe but also at an indoor or private playhouse in Blackfriars. This theater had been constructed in 1596 by James Burbage in an upper hall of a former Dominican priory or monastic house. Although Henry VIII had dissolved all English monasteries in the 1530s (shortly after he had founded the Church of England), the area remained under church, rather than hostile civic, control. The hall that Burbage had purchased and renovated was a large one in which Parliament had once met. In the private theater that he constructed, the stage, lit by candles, was built across the narrow end of the hall, with boxes flanking it. The rest of the hall offered seating room only. Because there was no provision for standing room, the largest audience it could hold was less than a thousand, or about a quarter of what the Globe could accommodate. Admission to Blackfriars was correspondingly more expensive. Instead of a penny to stand in the yard at the Globe, it cost a minimum of sixpence to get into Blackfriars. The best seats at the Globe (in the Lords' Room in the gallery above and behind the stage) cost sixpence; but the boxes flanking the stage at Blackfriars were half a crown, or five times sixpence. Some spectators who were particularly interested in displaying themselves paid even more to sit on stools on the Blackfriars stage.

Whether in the outdoor or indoor playhouses, the stages of Shakespeare's time were different from ours. They were not separated from the audience by the dropping of a curtain between acts and scenes. Therefore the playwrights of the time had to find other ways of signaling to the audience that one scene (to be imagined as occurring in one location at a given time) had ended and the next (to be imagined at perhaps a different location at a later time) had begun. The customary way used by Shakespeare and many of his contemporaries was to have everyone on stage exit at the end of one scene and have one or more different characters enter to begin the next. In a few cases, where characters remain onstage from one scene to another, the dialogue or stage action makes the change of location clear, and the characters are generally to be imagined as having moved from one place to another. For example, in *Romeo and Juliet*, Romeo and his friends remain onstage in Act 1 from scene 4 to scene 5, but they are represented as having moved between scenes from the street that leads to Capulet's house into Capulet's house itself. The new location is signaled in part by the appearance onstage of Capulet's servingmen carrying napkins, something they would not take into the streets. Playwrights had to be quite resourceful in the use of hand properties, like the napkin, or in the use of dialogue to specify where the action was taking place in their plays because, in contrast to most of today's theaters, the playhouses of Shakespeare's time did not use movable scenery to dress the stage and make the setting precise. As another consequence of this difference, however, the playwrights of Shakespeare's time did not have to specify exactly where the action of their plays was set when they did not choose to do so, and much of the action of their plays is tied to no specific place.

Usually Shakespeare's stage is referred to as a "bare stage," to distinguish it from the stages of the last two or three centuries with their elaborate sets. But the stage in Shakespeare's time was not completely bare. Philip Henslowe, owner of the Rose, lists in his inventory of stage properties a rock, three tombs, and two mossy banks. Stage directions in plays of the time also call for such things as thrones (or "states"), banquets (presumably tables with plaster replicas of food on them), and beds and tombs to be pushed onto the stage. Thus the stage often held more than the actors.

The actors did not limit their performing to the stage alone. Occasionally they went beneath the stage, as the Ghost appears to do in the first act of *Hamlet*. From there they could emerge onto the stage through a trapdoor. They could retire behind the hangings across the back of the stage (or the front of the tiring house), as, for example, the actor playing Polonius does when he hides behind the arras. Sometimes the hangings could be drawn back during a performance to "discover" one or more actors behind them. When performance required that an actor appear "above," as when Juliet is imagined to stand at the window of her chamber in the famous and misnamed "balcony scene," then the actor probably climbed the stairs to the gallery over the back of the stage and temporarily shared it with some of the spectators. The stage was also provided with ropes and winches so that actors could descend from, and reascend to, the "heavens."

Perhaps the greatest difference between dramatic performances in Shakespeare's time and ours was that in Shakespeare's England the roles of women were played by boys. (Some of these boys grew up to take male roles in their maturity.) There were no women in the acting companies, only in the audience. It had not always been so in the history of the English stage. There are records of women on English stages in the thirteenth and fourteenth centuries, two hundred years before Shakespeare's plays were performed. After the accession of James I in 1603, the queen of England and her ladies took part in entertainments at court called masques, and with the reopening of the theaters in 1660 at the restoration of Charles II, women again took their place on the public stage.

The chief competitors for the companies of adult actors such as the one to which Shakespeare belonged and for which he wrote were companies of exclusively boy actors. The competition was most intense in the early 1600s. There were then two principal children's companies: the Children of Paul's (the choirboys from St. Paul's Cathedral, whose private playhouse was near the cathedral); and the Children of the Chapel Royal (the choirboys from the monarch's private chapel, who performed at the Blackfriars theater built by Burbage in 1596, which Shakespeare's company had been stopped from using by local residents who objected to crowds). In *Hamlet* Shakespeare writes of "an aerie [nest] of children, little eyases [hawks], that cry out on the top of question and are most tyrannically clapped for 't. These are now the fashion and . . . berattle the common stages [attack the public theaters]." In the long run, the adult actors prevailed. The Children of Paul's dissolved around 1606. By about 1608 the Children of the Chapel Royal had been forced to stop playing at the Blackfriars theater, which was then taken over by the King's Men, Shakespeare's own troupe.

Acting companies and theaters of Shakespeare's time were organized in different ways. For example, Philip

Henslowe owned the Rose and leased it to companies of actors, who paid him from their takings. Henslowe would act as manager of these companies, initially paying playwrights for their plays and buying properties, recovering his outlay from the actors. Shakespeare's company, however, managed itself, with the principal actors, Shakespeare among them, having the status of "sharers" and the right to a share in the takings, as well as the responsibility for a part of the expenses. Five of the sharers themselves, Shakespeare among them, owned the Globe. As actor, as sharer in an acting company and in ownership of theaters, and as playwright, Shakespeare was about as involved in the theatrical industry as one could imagine. Although Shakespeare and his fellows prospered, their status under the law was conditional upon the protection of powerful patrons. "Common players"—those who did not have patrons or masters—were classed in the language of the law with "vagabonds and sturdy beggars." So the actors had to secure for themselves the official rank of servants of patrons. Among the patrons under whose protection Shakespeare's company worked were the lord chamberlain and, after the accession of King James in 1603, the king himself.

We are now perhaps on the verge of learning a great deal more about the theaters in which Shakespeare and his contemporaries performed—or at least of opening up new questions about them. Already about 70 percent of the Rose has been excavated, as has about 10 percent of the second Globe, the one built in 1614. It is to be hoped that soon more will be available for study. These are exciting times for students of Shakespeare's stage.

The Publication of Shakespeare's Plays

Eighteen of Shakespeare's plays found their way into print during the playwright's lifetime, but there is nothing to suggest that he took any interest in their publication. These eighteen appeared separately in editions called quartos. Their pages were not much larger than the one you are now reading, and these little books were sold unbound for a few pence. The earliest of the quartos that still survive were printed in 1594, the year that both *Titus Andronicus* and a version of the play now called *2 King Henry VI* became available. While almost every one of these early quartos displays on its title page the name of the acting company that performed the play, only about half provide the name of the playwright, Shakespeare. The first quarto edition to bear the name Shakespeare on its title page is *Love's Labor's Lost* of 1598. A few of these quartos were popular with the book-buying public of Shakespeare's lifetime; for example, quarto *Richard II* went through five editions between 1597 and 1615. But most of the quartos were far from best-sellers; *Love's Labor's Lost* (1598), for instance, was not reprinted in quarto until 1631. After Shakespeare's death, two more of his plays appeared in quarto format: *Othello* in 1622 and *The Two Noble Kinsmen*, coauthored with John Fletcher, in 1634.

In 1623, seven years after Shakespeare's death, *Mr. William Shakespeares Comedies, Histories, & Tragedies* was published. This printing offered readers in a single book thirty-six of the thirty-eight plays now thought to have been written by Shakespeare, including eighteen that had never been printed before. And it offered them in a style that was then reserved for serious literature and scholarship. The plays were arranged in double columns on pages nearly a foot high. This large page size is called "folio," as opposed to the smaller "quarto," and the 1623 volume is usually called the Shakespeare First Folio. It is reputed to have sold for the lordly price of a pound. (One copy at the Folger Library is marked fifteen shillings—that is, three-quarters of a pound.)

In a preface to the First Folio entitled "To the great Variety of Readers," two of Shakespeare's former fellow actors in the King's Men, John Heminge and Henry Condell, wrote that they themselves had collected their dead companion's plays. They suggested that they had seen his own papers: "we have scarce received from him a blot in his papers." The title page of the Folio declared that the plays within it had been printed "according to the True Original Copies." Comparing the Folio to the quartos, Heminge and Condell disparaged the quartos, advising their readers that "before you were abused with divers stolen and surreptitious copies, maimed, and deformed by the frauds and stealths of injurious impostors." Many Shakespeareans of the eighteenth and nineteenth centuries believed Heminge and Condell and regarded the Folio plays as superior to anything in the quartos.

Once we begin to examine the Folio plays in detail, it becomes less easy to take at face value the word of Heminge and Condell about the superiority of the Folio texts. For example, of the first nine plays in the Folio (one quarter of the entire collection), four were essentially reprinted from earlier quarto printings that Heminge and Condell had disparaged; and four have now been identified as printed from copies written in the hand of a professional scribe of the 1620s named Ralph Crane; the ninth, *The Comedy of Errors*, was apparently also printed from a manuscript, but one whose origin cannot be readily identified. Evidently then, eight of the first nine plays in the First Folio were not printed, in spite of what the Folio title page announces, "according to the True Original Copies," or Shakespeare's own papers, and the source of the ninth is unknown. Since today's editors have been forced to treat Heminge and Condell's pronouncements with skepticism, they must choose whether to base their own editions upon quartos or the Folio on grounds other than Heminge and Condell's story of where the quarto and Folio versions originated.

Editors have often fashioned their own narratives to explain what lies behind the quartos and Folio. They have said that Heminge and Condell meant to criticize only a few of the early quartos, the ones that offer much shorter and sometimes quite different, often garbled, versions of plays. Among the examples of these are the 1600 quarto of *Henry V* (the Folio offers a much fuller version) or the 1603 *Hamlet* quarto (in 1604 a different, much longer form of the play got into print as a quarto). Early in this century editors speculated that these questionable texts were produced when someone in the audience took notes from the plays' dialogue during performances and then employed "hack poets" to fill out the notes. The poor results were then sold to a publisher and presented in print as Shakespeare's plays. More recently this story has given way to another in which the shorter versions are said to be recreations from memory of Shakespeare's plays by actors who wanted to stage them in the provinces but lacked manuscript copies. Most of the quartos offer much better texts than these so-called bad quartos. Indeed, in most of the quartos we find texts that are at least equal to or better than what is printed in the Folio. Many of this century's Shakespeare enthusiasts have persuaded themselves that most of the quartos were set into type directly from Shakespeare's own papers, although there is nothing on which to base this conclusion except the desire for it to be true. Thus speculation continues about how the Shakespeare plays got to be printed. All that we have are the printed texts.

The book collector who was most successful in bringing together copies of the quartos and the First Folio was Henry Clay Folger, founder of the Folger Shakespeare Library in Washington, D.C. While it is estimated that there survive around the world only about 230 copies of the First Folio, Mr. Folger was able to acquire more than seventy-five copies, as well as a large number of fragments, for the library that bears his name. He also amassed a substantial number of quartos. For example, only fourteen copies of the First Quarto of *Love's Labor's Lost* are known to exist, and three are at the Folger Shakespeare Library. As a consequence of Mr. Folger's labors, twentieth-century scholars visiting the Folger Library have been able to learn a great deal about sixteenth- and seventeenth-century printing and, particularly, about the printing of Shakespeare's plays. And Mr. Folger did not stop at the First Folio, but collected many copies of later editions of Shakespeare, beginning with the Second Folio (1632), the Third (1663–64), and the Fourth (1685). Each of these later folios was based on its immediate predecessor and was edited anonymously. The first editor of Shakespeare whose name we know was Nicholas Rowe, whose first edition came out in 1709. Mr. Folger collected this edition and many, many more by Rowe's successors.

An Introduction to This Text

The Merchant of Venice was first printed in 1600 as a quarto. Then in 1619 someone edited a copy of the 1600 quarto to make it the basis of a second quarto-edition of the play. But whoever did the editing for this 1619 quarto does not seem to have had access to either an author's manuscript or one from the theater and does not even seem always to have understood the play. In 1623 the play was again printed, this time as a part of the collection of Shakespeare's plays now known as the First Folio. Like the Second Quarto of 1619, the First Folio text is based on an edited copy of the First Quarto of 1600. Some scholars think that whoever did the editing for the First Folio *Merchant of Venice* must have referred to a manuscript of the play that had been used in the theater, but this theory is not well founded.

The present edition is based directly on the earliest quarto of 1600.* For the convenience of the reader, we have modernized the punctuation and the spelling of the quarto. Sometimes we go so far as to modernize certain old forms of words; for example, when *a* means "he," we change it to *he;* we change *mo* to *more,* and *ye* to *you.* But it is not our practice in editing any of the plays to modernize words that sound distinctly different from modern forms. For example, when the early printed texts read *sith* or *apricocks* or *porpentine,* we have not modernized to *since, apricots, porcupine.* When the forms *an, and,* or *and if* appear instead of

---

*We have also consulted the computerized text of the First Quarto provided by the Text Archive of the Oxford University Computing Centre, to which we are grateful.

the modern form *if*, we have reduced *and* to *an* but have not changed any of these forms to their modern equivalent, *if*. We also modernize and, where necessary, correct passages in foreign languages, unless an error in the early printed text can be reasonably explained as a joke.

Whenever we change the wording of the First Quarto or add anything to its stage directions, we mark the change by enclosing it in superior half-brackets (⌐ ¬). We want our readers to be immediately aware when we have intervened. (Only when we correct an obvious typographical error in the First Quarto does the change not get marked.) Whenever we change either the First Quarto's wording or its punctuation so that its meaning changes, we list the change in the textual notes at the back of the book, even if all we have done is fix an obvious error.

We correct or regularize a number of the proper names. For example, the first time that the play's clown, Lancelet Gobbo, comes on stage, he calls himself "Launcelet Iobbe." Then his father enters under the name "old Gobbo." Like most editors before us, we think that the father and son had the same last name, which we spell "Gobbo." Unlike all modern editors, however, we retain the First Quarto's name "Lancelet" for the clown rather than changing it to "Lancelot." Editors and readers have often had trouble distinguishing among three characters with closely similar names: Salarino, Solanio, and Salerio. Ever since 1926 when John Dover Wilson argued that Shakespeare had thought of Salarino and Salerio as the same character, all editors (except Professor M. M. Mahood) have collapsed the three characters into two named Salerio and Solanio. We acknowledge that in one scene (Act 3, scene 3) there is a confusion involving the name Salerio, but we do not think that this single confusion is enough to warrant collapsing the three roles into two. We do regularize the name Salarino, which is sometimes spelled "Salaryno" or "Salerino" as well as "Salarino" in the First Quarto.

This edition differs from many earlier ones in its efforts to aid the reader in imagining the play as a performance rather than as a series of fictional events. Thus stage directions are written with reference to the stage. For example, at the very end of the play Nerissa says that she is giving Lorenzo "a special deed of gift," and so she is in the fiction of the play. Yet on stage the actor playing Nerissa would not hand over a "deed" but simply a piece of paper. Therefore, instead of following other editors in printing a stage direction that reads *"Handing him a deed,"* we print *"Handing him a paper."* Whenever it is reasonably certain, in our view, that a speech is accompanied by a particular action, we provide a stage direction describing the action. (Occasional exceptions to this rule occur when the action is so obvious that to add a stage direction would insult the reader.) Stage directions for the entrance of characters in mid-scene are, with rare exceptions, placed so that they immediately precede the characters' participation in the scene, even though these entrances may appear somewhat earlier in the early printed texts. Whenever we move a stage direction, we record this change in the textual notes. Latin stage directions (e.g., *Exeunt*) are translated into English (e.g., *They exit*).

We expand the often severely abbreviated forms of names used as speech headings in early printed texts into the full names of the characters. We also regularize the speakers' names in speech headings, using only a single designation for each character, even though the early printed texts sometimes use a variety of designations. Variations in the speech headings of the early printed texts are recorded in the textual notes.

In the present edition, as well, we mark with a dash any change of address within a speech, unless a stage direction intervenes. When the *-ed* ending of a word is to be pronounced, we mark it with an accent. Like editors for the last two centuries, we print metrically linked lines in the following way:

> PORTIA
>   Is your name Shylock?
> SHYLOCK   Shylock is my name.

However, when there are a number of short verse-lines that can be linked in more than one way, we do not, with rare exceptions, indent any of them.

The Explanatory Notes

The notes that appear on the pages facing the text are designed to provide readers with the help that they may need to enjoy the play. Whenever the meaning of a word in the text is not readily accessible in a good contemporary dictionary, we offer the meaning in a note. Sometimes we provide a note even when the relevant meaning is to be found in the dictionary but when the word has acquired since Shakespeare's time other potentially confusing meanings. In our notes, we try to offer modern synonyms for Shakespeare's words. We also try to indicate to the reader the connection between the word in the play and the modern synonym. For example, Shakespeare sometimes uses the word *head* to mean "source," but, for modern readers, there may be no connection evident between these two words. We provide the connection by explaining Shakespeare's usage as follows: "**head:** fountainhead, source." On some occasions, a whole phrase or clause needs explanation. Then we rephrase in our own words the difficult passage, and add at the end synonyms for individual words in the passage. When scholars have been unable to determine the meaning of a word or phrase, we acknowledge the uncertainty.

THE
MERCHANT
OF
VENICE

Characters in the Play

PORTIA, an heiress of Belmont
NERISSA, her waiting-gentlewoman
BALTHAZAR } *servants to Portia*
STEPHANO

Prince of MOROCCO } *suitors to Portia*
Prince of ARRAGON

ANTONIO, a merchant of Venice
BASSANIO, a Venetian gentleman, suitor to Portia
SOLANIO
SALARINO
GRATIANO } *companions of Antonio and Bassanio*
LORENZO
LEONARDO, servant to Bassanio

SHYLOCK, a Jewish moneylender in Venice
JESSICA, his daughter
TUBAL, another Jewish moneylender
LANCELET GOBBO, servant to Shylock and later to Bassanio
OLD GOBBO, Lancelet's father

SALERIO, a messenger from Venice
Jailer
Duke of Venice

Magnificoes of Venice
Servants
Attendants and followers
Messenger
Musicians

3

THE
MERCHANT
OF
VENICE

ACT 1

1.1 Antonio, a Venetian merchant, has invested all his wealth in trading expeditions. Bassanio, his friend and kinsman, asks him for money to go to Belmont, where Bassanio hopes to marry the heiress Portia. Antonio gives Bassanio permission to borrow the money on Antonio's credit.

———

1. **sooth:** truth
5. **I am to learn:** i.e., I do not know
6. **want-wit:** fool
7. **ado:** difficulty, trouble
9. **argosies:** large merchant ships; **portly:** fat-bellied; stately
10. **signiors:** Venetian noblemen; **flood:** water
11. **pageants:** floats in street processions; elaborately decorated barges
12. **overpeer:** look down on; **petty traffickers:** i.e., smaller ships
13. **do them reverence:** curtsy or bow to them
14. **they:** i.e., the argosies
15. **venture:** commercial enterprise involving risk (specifically, for Antonio, his ships and their cargoes of **spices** [line 34] and **silks** [line 35]); **forth:** abroad
16. **The better part:** most; **affections:** feelings
17. **still:** always
19. **Piring:** peering; **roads:** places to anchor

⌜ACT 1⌝

⌜Scene 1⌝

Enter Antonio, Salarino, and Solanio.

ANTONIO
  In sooth I know not why I am so sad.
  It wearies me, you say it wearies you.
  But how I caught it, found it, or came by it,
  What stuff 'tis made of, whereof it is born,
  I am to learn.   5
  And such a want-wit sadness makes of me
  That I have much ado to know myself.

SALARINO
  Your mind is tossing on the ocean,
  There where your argosies with portly sail
  (Like signiors and rich burghers on the flood,   10
  Or, as it were, the pageants of the sea)
  Do overpeer the petty traffickers
  That curtsy to them, do them reverence,
  As they fly by them with their woven wings.

SOLANIO
  Believe me, sir, had I such venture forth,   15
  The better part of my affections would
  Be with my hopes abroad. I should be still
  Plucking the grass to know where sits the wind,
  Piring in maps for ports and piers and roads;
  And every object that might make me fear   20

21. **out of doubt:** certainly

23. **wind:** i.e., breath

24. **blow me to an ague:** give me chills and fever

27. **flats:** shoals

28. **wealthy Andrew:** a ship with a rich cargo, like the Spanish ship *San Andres* (or *Andrew*) captured by the English at Cadiz in 1596

29. **Vailing:** lowering

32. **bethink me straight:** think immediately

36–37. **but even now . . . worth nothing:** i.e., one minute worth a lot, the next minute worth nothing

39. **thing bechanced:** possibility

43. **bottom:** ship's hull or bottom; also, ship, as in the proverb "Venture not all in one bottom"

52–53. **two-headed Janus:** the Roman god with two faces looking in opposite directions

Janus. (1.1.53)
From Andrea Alciati, *Emblemata . . .* (1583).

Misfortune to my ventures, out of doubt
Would make me sad.

SALARINO   My wind cooling my broth
Would blow me to an ague when I thought
What harm a wind too great might do at sea.   25
I should not see the sandy hourglass run
But I should think of shallows and of flats,
And see my wealthy *Andrew* ⌈docked⌉ in sand,
Vailing her high top lower than her ribs
To kiss her burial. Should I go to church   30
And see the holy edifice of stone
And not bethink me straight of dangerous rocks,
Which, touching but my gentle vessel's side,
Would scatter all her spices on the stream,
Enrobe the roaring waters with my silks,   35
And, in a word, but even now worth this
And now worth nothing? Shall I have the thought
To think on this, and shall I lack the thought
That such a thing bechanced would make me sad?
But tell not me: I know Antonio   40
Is sad to think upon his merchandise.

ANTONIO

Believe me, no. I thank my fortune for it,
My ventures are not in one bottom trusted,
Nor to one place; nor is my whole estate
Upon the fortune of this present year: 45
Therefore my merchandise makes me not sad.

SOLANIO

Why then you are in love.

ANTONIO   Fie, fie!

SOLANIO

Not in love neither? Then let us say you are sad
Because you are not merry; and 'twere as easy   50
For you to laugh and leap, and say you are merry
Because you are not sad. Now, by two-headed
    Janus,

57. **other:** i.e., others; **vinegar aspect:** sour face (accent **aspect** on second syllable)

59. **Nestor:** the wise old Greek councillor

60. **kinsman:** This is the only place in the play that such a family relationship is mentioned.

71. **grow exceeding strange:** i.e., are becoming complete strangers

72. **We'll make . . . on yours:** i.e., we'll find time for you whenever you are available

78. **have . . . upon:** i.e., pay too much attention to

A merchant of Venice.
From Jean de Glen, *Des habits, moeurs* . . . (1601).

Nature hath framed strange fellows in her time:
Some that will evermore peep through their eyes   55
And laugh like parrots at a bagpiper,
And other of such vinegar aspect
That they'll not show their teeth in way of smile
Though Nestor swear the jest be laughable.

Enter Bassanio, Lorenzo, and Gratiano.

Here comes Bassanio, your most noble kinsman,   60
Gratiano, and Lorenzo. Fare you well.
We leave you now with better company.

SALARINO
I would have stayed till I had made you merry,
If worthier friends had not prevented me.

ANTONIO
Your worth is very dear in my regard.   65
I take it your own business calls on you,
And you embrace th' occasion to depart.

SALARINO
Good morrow, my good lords.

BASSANIO
Good signiors both, when shall we laugh? Say,
  when?   70
You grow exceeding strange. Must it be so?

SALARINO
We'll make our leisures to attend on yours.
                          Salarino and Solanio exit.

LORENZO
My Lord Bassanio, since you have found Antonio,
We two will leave you. But at dinner time
I pray you have in mind where we must meet.   75

BASSANIO
I will not fail you.

GRATIANO
You look not well, Signior Antonio.
You have too much respect upon the world.

81. **hold:** i.e., regard, value

85. **old wrinkles:** i.e., (1) wrinkles that come with age; (2) many wrinkles, from laughing

87. **mortifying:** self-denying; life-destroying

89. **his . . . alabaster:** the tomb-sculpture of his grandfather

90–91. **creep . . . peevish:** contract jaundice through bad temper (Jaundice was believed to result from an excess of bile, which made one **peevish**.)

94. **cream and mantle:** i.e., acquire a covering (**mantle**) of scum (**cream**)

95. **stillness:** silence; **entertain:** adopt

96. **opinion:** reputation

97. **conceit:** thought

98. **As who should:** i.e., as if he would

103–5. **would . . . fools:** i.e., by speaking, they would put their audience in danger of damnation (According to Matthew 5.22, "Whosoever shall say [to his brother], 'Thou fool,' shall be in danger of hell-fire.")

107. **melancholy bait:** i.e., bait of melancholy

108. **gudgeon:** a fish said to swallow anything

112. **dumb:** silent

They lose it that do buy it with much care.
Believe me, you are marvelously changed.   80
ANTONIO
I hold the world but as the world, Gratiano,
A stage where every man must play a part,
And mine a sad one.
GRATIANO   Let me play the fool.
With mirth and laughter let old wrinkles come,   85
And let my liver rather heat with wine
Than my heart cool with mortifying groans.
Why should a man whose blood is warm within
Sit like his grandsire cut in alabaster?
Sleep when he wakes? And creep into the jaundice   90
By being peevish? I tell thee what, Antonio
(I love thee, and 'tis my love that speaks):
There are a sort of men whose visages
Do cream and mantle like a standing pond
And do a willful stillness entertain   95
With purpose to be dressed in an opinion
Of wisdom, gravity, profound conceit,
As who should say "I am Sir Oracle,
And when I ope my lips, let no dog bark."
O my Antonio, I do know of these   100
That therefore only are reputed wise
For saying nothing, when, I am very sure,
If they should speak, would almost damn those ears
Which, hearing them, would call their brothers
    fools.   105
I'll tell thee more of this another time.
But fish not with this melancholy bait
For this fool gudgeon, this opinion.—
Come, good Lorenzo.—Fare you well a while.
I'll end my exhortation after dinner.   110
LORENZO
Well, we will leave you then till dinner time.
I must be one of these same dumb wise men,
For Gratiano never lets me speak.

117. **for this gear:** because of this speech

119. **neat's:** ox's; **maid not vendible:** a woman who cannot be sold on the marriage market

120. **that:** i.e., Gratiano's speech

124. **shall:** must; **ere:** before

126. **the same:** i.e., the one

130. **disabled:** i.e., depleted

131–32. **By something . . . grant continuance:** i.e., by displaying a rather more grand style of life than my modest means would allow me to continue

133–34. **make moan . . . rate:** complain about being forced to cut back on this great expenditure

135. **come . . . debts:** discharge with honor the large debts

136. **time:** i.e., past

137. **gaged:** obliged (to pay)

139. **from . . . warranty:** i.e., your love gives me authorization

140. **unburden:** i.e., reveal

GRATIANO
  Well, keep me company but two years more,
  Thou shalt not know the sound of thine own   115
    tongue.
ANTONIO
  Fare you well. I'll grow a talker for this gear.
GRATIANO
  Thanks, i' faith, for silence is only commendable
  In a neat's tongue dried and a maid not vendible.
                    ⌜*Gratiano and Lorenzo*⌝ *exit.*
ANTONIO   Is that anything now?   120
BASSANIO   Gratiano speaks an infinite deal of nothing,
    more than any man in all Venice. His reasons are as
    two grains of wheat hid in two bushels of chaff: you
    shall seek all day ere you find them, and when you
    have them, they are not worth the search.   125
ANTONIO
  Well, tell me now what lady is the same
  To whom you swore a secret pilgrimage,
  That you today promised to tell me of?
BASSANIO
  'Tis not unknown to you, Antonio,
  How much I have disabled mine estate   130
  By something showing a more swelling port
  Than my faint means would grant continuance.
  Nor do I now make moan to be abridged
  From such a noble rate. But my chief care
  Is to come fairly off from the great debts   135
  Wherein my time, something too prodigal,
  Hath left me gaged. To you, Antonio,
  I owe the most in money and in love,
  And from your love I have a warranty
  To unburden all my plots and purposes   140
  How to get clear of all the debts I owe.
ANTONIO
  I pray you, good Bassanio, let me know it;

146. **to your occasions:** for your needs

147. **shaft:** arrow

148. **his fellow:** i.e., another; **the selfsame flight:** i.e., the same weight and size

151. **proof:** experience

155. **self:** i.e., selfsame, same

157–58. **or . . . Or:** i.e., either . . . or

158. **latter hazard:** second venture

160. **spend but time:** i.e., waste time

161. **To wind about . . . with circumstance:** i.e., to go so indirectly; to argue circumstantially

162. **out of doubt:** certainly

163. **making question of my uttermost:** i.e., doubting that I would do everything I could for you

167. **prest:** ready (French *prêt*)

168. **richly left:** i.e., who has inherited riches

170. **Sometimes:** formerly, once

172–73. **nothing . . . To:** i.e., of no less worth

173. **Cato's . . . Portia:** The historical Portia was daughter to the Roman statesman Cato and wife to Brutus, leader of the conspiracy against Julius Caesar.

"The four winds." (1.1.175)
From Giulio Capaccio, *Delle imprese trattato . . .* (1592).

And if it stand, as you yourself still do,
Within the eye of honor, be assured
My purse, my person, my extremest means   145
Lie all unlocked to your occasions.

BASSANIO
In my school days, when I had lost one shaft,
I shot his fellow of the selfsame flight
The selfsame way with more advisèd watch
To find the other forth; and by adventuring both   150
I oft found both. I urge this childhood proof
Because what follows is pure innocence.
I owe you much, and, like a willful youth,
That which I owe is lost. But if you please
To shoot another arrow that self way   155
Which you did shoot the first, I do not doubt,
As I will watch the aim, or to find both
Or bring your latter hazard back again,
And thankfully rest debtor for the first.

ANTONIO
You know me well, and herein spend but time   160
To wind about my love with circumstance;
And out of doubt you do me now more wrong
In making question of my uttermost
Than if you had made waste of all I have.
Then do but say to me what I should do   165
That in your knowledge may by me be done,
And I am prest unto it. Therefore speak.

BASSANIO
In Belmont is a lady richly left,
And she is fair, and, fairer than that word,
Of wondrous virtues. Sometimes from her eyes   170
I did receive fair speechless messages.
Her name is Portia, nothing undervalued
To Cato's daughter, Brutus' Portia.
Nor is the wide world ignorant of her worth,
For the four winds blow in from every coast   175

178. **Colchos' strond:** the shore of Colchos on the Black Sea where, in Greek mythology, Jason and the Argonauts went in quest of the Golden Fleece

180–81. **means . . . one of them:** i.e., the wealth to stand on equal footing with one of Portia's suitors

182. **presages me:** forecasts to me; **thrift:** success

183. **questionless:** unquestionably

185. **commodity:** goods, i.e., collateral

188. **racked:** strained

189. **furnish thee to:** equip you to journey to

190. **presently:** immediately

191–92. **I . . . sake:** i.e., I have no doubt that I will get it either on my credit as a merchant or from friends

1.2 At Portia's estate of Belmont, Portia and Nerissa talk over Portia's frustration at being unable to choose her own husband. According to her father's will, she may marry only the man who chooses correctly among three small chests made of gold, silver, and lead. Portia likes none of the suitors who have so far arrived. A messenger enters to announce the coming of a new suitor, the Prince of Morocco.

---

1. **By my troth:** a mild oath like "Upon my word"

5. **aught:** anything

6. **surfeit:** overindulge

7. **mean:** small, inconsiderable

7–8. **to be seated in the mean:** i.e., to be located in the middle between excess and want

8. **Superfluity:** excess

(continued)

Renownèd suitors, and her sunny locks
Hang on her temples like a golden fleece,
Which makes her seat of Belmont Colchos' strond,
And many Jasons come in quest of her.
O my Antonio, had I but the means   180
To hold a rival place with one of them,
I have a mind presages me such thrift
That I should questionless be fortunate!

ANTONIO
Thou know'st that all my fortunes are at sea;
Neither have I money nor commodity   185
To raise a present sum. Therefore go forth:
Try what my credit can in Venice do;
That shall be racked even to the uttermost
To furnish thee to Belmont to fair Portia.
Go presently inquire, and so will I,   190
Where money is, and I no question make
To have it of my trust, or for my sake.

⌜They exit.⌝

⌜Scene 2⌝
Enter Portia with her waiting woman Nerissa.

PORTIA   By my troth, Nerissa, my little body is aweary
of this great world.

NERISSA   You would be, sweet madam, if your miseries
were in the same abundance as your good fortunes
are. And yet, for aught I see, they are as sick that   5
surfeit with too much as they that starve with
nothing. It is no mean happiness, therefore, to be
seated in the mean. Superfluity comes sooner by
white hairs, but competency lives longer.

PORTIA   Good sentences, and well pronounced.   10

NERISSA   They would be better if well followed.

8–9. **comes . . . hairs:** i.e., ages the person more quickly

9. **competency:** sufficiency

10. **sentences:** sayings (Latin *sententiae*); **pronounced:** delivered

14. **divine:** clergyman

18. **blood:** i.e., emotions, feelings

20. **meshes:** nets used in pursuit of hares

21. **in the fashion:** i.e., of the sort

30. **whereof:** i.e., whereby; **who:** whoever; **his:** i.e., your father's

36. **overname them:** say their names over

38. **level:** aim at; guess

41–42. **appropriation:** addition

42. **good parts:** achievements

44. **played false:** i.e., committed adultery; **smith:** blacksmith

45. **County:** count

46. **as who should say:** i.e., as much as to say

47. **An:** i.e., if; **choose:** do as you please

PORTIA If to do were as easy as to know what were
good to do, chapels had been churches, and poor
men's cottages princes' palaces. It is a good divine
that follows his own instructions. I can easier teach   15
twenty what were good to be done than to be one of
the twenty to follow mine own teaching. The brain
may devise laws for the blood, but a hot temper
leaps o'er a cold decree: such a hare is madness the
youth, to skip o'er the meshes of good counsel the   20
cripple. But this reasoning is not in the fashion to
choose me a husband. O, me, the word "choose"! I
may neither choose who I would nor refuse who I
dislike. So is the will of a living daughter curbed by
the will of a dead father. Is it not hard, Nerissa, that   25
I cannot choose one, nor refuse none?

NERISSA Your father was ever virtuous, and holy men
at their death have góod inspirations. Therefore the
lottery that he hath devised in these three chests of
gold, silver, and lead, whereof who chooses his   30
meaning chooses you, will no doubt never be
chosen by any rightly but one who you shall rightly
love. But what warmth is there in your affection
towards any of these princely suitors that are already come?   35

PORTIA I pray thee, overname them, and as thou
namest them, I will describe them, and according
to my description level at my affection.

NERISSA First, there is the Neapolitan prince.

PORTIA Ay, that's a colt indeed, for he doth nothing but   40
talk of his horse, and he makes it a great appropriation to his own good parts that he can shoe him
himself. I am much afeard my lady his mother
played false with a smith.

NERISSA Then is there the County Palatine.   45

PORTIA He doth nothing but frown, as who should say
"An you will not have me, choose." He hears

49. **weeping philosopher:** Heraclitus of Ephesus, who wept at people's consuming desire for riches

51. **death's-head:** skull

54. **How say you by:** i.e., what do you say about

61. **throstle:** thrush; **straight:** immediately; **a-cap'ring:** dancing

64–65. **to madness:** madly

70–71. **come . . . swear:** i.e., bear witness

71–72. **have . . . English:** i.e., speak little English

72. **proper man's picture:** i.e., the picture of an ideal man

73. **dumb show:** i.e., someone who does not speak (literally, a part of a play presented without speech)

74. **suited:** dressed; **doublet:** jacket

75. **round hose:** wide breeches

80–82. **he borrowed . . . able:** i.e., he let the Englishman slap his ear and, instead of defending himself, swore that he'd pay him back later

82–83. **became . . . another:** perhaps, guaranteed that the Scot would pay back the Englishman and promised to add his own blow as well; or, perhaps, let the Englishman slap his ear as well, promising to retaliate

merry tales and smiles not. I fear he will prove the
weeping philosopher when he grows old, being so
full of unmannerly sadness in his youth. I had   50
rather be married to a death's-head with a bone in
his mouth than to either of these. God defend me
from these two!

NERISSA   How say you by the French lord, Monsieur Le
⌈Bon⌉?   55

PORTIA   God made him, and therefore let him pass for
a man. In truth, I know it is a sin to be a mocker,
but he!—why, he hath a horse better than the
Neapolitan's, a better bad habit of frowning than
the Count Palatine. He is every man in no man. If a   60
⌈throstle⌉ sing, he falls straight a-cap'ring. He will
fence with his own shadow. If I should marry him, I
should marry twenty husbands! If he would despise
me, I would forgive him, for if he love me to
madness, I shall never requite him.   65

NERISSA   What say you then to Falconbridge, the young
baron of England?

PORTIA   You know I say nothing to him, for he understands not me, nor I him. He hath neither Latin,
French, nor Italian; and you will come into the   70
court and swear that I have a poor pennyworth in
the English. He is a proper man's picture, but alas,
who can converse with a dumb show? How oddly
he is suited! I think he bought his doublet in Italy,
his round hose in France, his bonnet in Germany,   75
and his behavior everywhere.

NERISSA   What think you of the Scottish lord, his
neighbor?

PORTIA   That he hath a neighborly charity in him, for
he borrowed a box of the ear of the Englishman,   80
and swore he would pay him again when he was
able. I think the Frenchman became his surety and
sealed under for another.

89–90. **An ... fall:** if the worst befall, happen

90. **make shift:** i.e., find a way

93. **casket:** small ornamental chest for holding jewels and other valuables

96. **deep:** i.e., tall; **contrary:** wrong

104. **by some other sort:** i.e., in some other way

105. **imposition:** order, command

106. **Sibylla:** the Sybil of Cumae, to whom Apollo granted as many years of life as there are grains in a handful of sand

107. **Diana:** goddess of chastity

Diana. (1.2.107)
From Robert Whitcombe, *Janua diuorum* ... (1678).

NERISSA How like you the young German, the Duke of
Saxony's nephew? 85

PORTIA Very vilely in the morning, when he is sober,
and most vilely in the afternoon, when he is drunk.
When he is best he is a little worse than a man, and
when he is worst he is little better than a beast. An
the worst fall that ever fell, I hope I shall make shift 90
to go without him.

NERISSA If he should offer to choose, and choose the
right casket, you should refuse to perform your
father's will if you should refuse to accept him.

PORTIA Therefore, for fear of the worst, I pray thee set 95
a deep glass of Rhenish wine on the contrary
casket, for if the devil be within and that tempta-
tion without, I know he will choose it. I will do
anything, Nerissa, ere I will be married to a sponge.

NERISSA You need not fear, lady, the having any of 100
these lords. They have acquainted me with their
determinations, which is indeed to return to their
home and to trouble you with no more suit, unless
you may be won by some other sort than your
father's imposition depending on the caskets. 105

PORTIA If I live to be as old as Sibylla, I will die as
chaste as Diana unless I be obtained by the manner
of my father's will. I am glad this parcel of wooers
are so reasonable, for there is not one among them
but I dote on his very absence. And I pray God 110
grant them a fair departure!

NERISSA Do you not remember, lady, in your father's
time, a Venetian, a scholar and a soldier, that came
hither in company of the Marquess of Montferrat?

PORTIA Yes, yes, it was Bassanio—as I think so was he 115
called.

NERISSA True, madam. He, of all the men that ever my
foolish eyes looked upon, was the best deserving a
fair lady.

129. **condition:** character
131. **shrive me:** grant me absolution
132. **Sirrah:** a term of address to a male social inferior

1.3 In Venice Bassanio goes to Shylock, a Jewish moneylender, to borrow, in Antonio's name, 3000 ducats. Shylock hates Antonio but agrees to lend the money provided that Antonio sign a bond to yield a pound of his own flesh if he is unable to repay the loan on time. Shylock insists that the bond is a kind of joke, a "merry bond." Bassanio distrusts Shylock, but Antonio, confident of the success of his trading expeditions, agrees to sign the bond.

————————

1. **ducats:** Venetian gold coins
5. **bound:** i.e., obligated by a legal bond to repay
7. **May you stead:** can you help; **pleasure:** gratify

PORTIA   I remember him well, and I remember him   120
   worthy of thy praise.

               Enter a Servingman.

   How now, what news?

SERVINGMAN   The four strangers seek for you, madam,
   to take their leave. And there is a forerunner come
   from a fifth, the Prince of Morocco, who brings   125
   word the Prince his master will be here tonight.

PORTIA   If I could bid the fifth welcome with so good
   heart as I can bid the other four farewell, I should
   be glad of his approach. If he have the condition of
   a saint and the complexion of a devil, I had rather   130
   he should shrive me than wive me.
   Come, Nerissa. ⌜*To Servingman.*⌝ Sirrah, go before.—
   Whiles we shut the gate upon one wooer, another
   knocks at the door.

                      They exit.

               ⌜Scene 3⌝
     Enter Bassanio with Shylock the Jew.

SHYLOCK   Three thousand ducats, well.
BASSANIO   Ay, sir, for three months.
SHYLOCK   For three months, well.
BASSANIO   For the which, as I told you, Antonio shall
   be bound.   5
SHYLOCK   Antonio shall become bound, well.
BASSANIO   May you stead me? Will you pleasure me?
   Shall I know your answer?
SHYLOCK   Three thousand ducats for three months,
   and Antonio bound.   10
BASSANIO   Your answer to that?
SHYLOCK   Antonio is a good man.
BASSANIO   Have you heard any imputation to the con-
   trary?

17. **sufficient:** i.e., as a guarantee or security; **in supposition:** uncertain

19. **Rialto:** the Exchange, where merchants gathered

21. **squandered:** scattered (perhaps imprudently)

28. **assured:** satisfied (Shylock, in the following line, uses **assured** to mean "financially guaranteed.")

33–35. **the habitation . . . into:** The gospels (Matthew 8.28–32, Mark 5.1–13, and Luke 8.27–33) describe Christ (**your prophet the Nazarite**) driving devils out of madmen and into a herd of swine.

41. **publican:** collector of Roman taxes and enemy of the Jews (In Luke 18.9–14, Jesus tells of a publican whose humility justified him in God's eyes.)

42. **for:** because

43. **low simplicity:** humble foolishness

44. **gratis:** without interest

45. **usance:** interest

46. **catch him . . . the hip:** have him at my mercy (The term comes from wrestling.)

SHYLOCK   Ho, no, no, no, no! My meaning in saying he   15
   is a good man is to have you understand me that he
   is sufficient. Yet his means are in supposition: he
   hath an argosy bound to Tripolis, another to the
   Indies. I understand, moreover, upon the Rialto,
   he hath a third at Mexico, a fourth for England, and   20
   other ventures he hath squandered abroad. But
   ships are but boards, sailors but men; there be land
   rats and water rats, water thieves and land
   thieves—I mean pirates—and then there is the
   peril of waters, winds, and rocks. The man is,   25
   notwithstanding, sufficient. Three thousand ducats.
   I think I may take his bond.
BASSANIO   Be assured you may.
SHYLOCK   I will be assured I may. And that I may be
   assured, I will bethink me. May I speak with   30
   Antonio?
BASSANIO   If it please you to dine with us.
SHYLOCK   Yes, to smell pork! To eat of the habitation
   which your prophet the Nazarite conjured the
   devil into! I will buy with you, sell with you, talk   35
   with you, walk with you, and so following; but I
   will not eat with you, drink with you, nor pray with
   you.—What news on the Rialto?—Who is he comes
   here?

Enter Antonio.

BASSANIO   This is Signior Antonio.   40
SHYLOCK, ⌜*aside*⌝
   How like a fawning publican he looks!
   I hate him for he is a Christian,
   But more for that in low simplicity
   He lends out money gratis and brings down
   The rate of usance here with us in Venice.   45
   If I can catch him once upon the hip,
   I will feed fat the ancient grudge I bear him.

50. **thrift:** profit, gains

54. **debating . . . store:** i.e., considering how much ready cash I have

59. **soft:** i.e., wait a minute

60. **Rest you fair:** a polite greeting

62. **Your Worship . . . mouths:** i.e., we were just now speaking of you

64. **excess:** i.e., interest

65. **ripe wants:** i.e., urgent needs

66–67. **Is he yet possessed:** i.e., does he yet know

68. **would:** i.e., would have

76. **Methoughts:** I thought

77. **Upon advantage:** i.e., with interest

78. **I do never use it:** i.e., that is not my practice

79–98. Shylock tells the story (found in Genesis 30.25–43) of Jacob, who, serving Laban for seven years in order to win Laban's daughter Rachel, contracted with Laban to take as wages only the multicolored lambs born that year. When the ewes were in heat, Jacob drove into the ground before them branches with the bark peeled partway back (multicolored branches) so that, in the act of copulation, the ewes would see them. It was believed that offspring resembled whatever the mother saw at conception. Jacob thereby acquired a great flock.

He hates our sacred nation, and he rails,
Even there where merchants most do congregate,
On me, my bargains, and my well-won thrift,   50
Which he calls "interest." Cursèd be my tribe
If I forgive him!
BASSANIO   Shylock, do you hear?
SHYLOCK
I am debating of my present store,
And, by the near guess of my memory,   55
I cannot instantly raise up the gross
Of full three thousand ducats. What of that?
Tubal, a wealthy Hebrew of my tribe,
Will furnish me. But soft, how many months
Do you desire? ⌜*To Antonio.*⌝ Rest you fair, good   60
    signior!
Your Worship was the last man in our mouths.
ANTONIO
Shylock, albeit I neither lend nor borrow
By taking nor by giving of excess,
Yet, to supply the ripe wants of my friend,   65
I'll break a custom. ⌜*To Bassanio.*⌝ Is he yet
    possessed
How much you would?
SHYLOCK   Ay, ay, three thousand
    ducats.   70
ANTONIO   And for three months.
SHYLOCK   I had forgot—three months. ⌜*To Bassanio.*⌝
    You told me so.—
Well then, your bond. And let me see—but hear
    you: 75
Methoughts you said you neither lend nor borrow
Upon advantage.
ANTONIO   I do never use it.
SHYLOCK
When Jacob grazed his Uncle Laban's sheep—
This Jacob from our holy Abram was   80

81. **wrought:** managed (Genesis 27 describes how Rebecca, Jacob's mother, tricked her husband, Isaac, into making Jacob his heir.)

82. **third possessor:** Jacob inherited from Isaac, who had inherited from Abraham.

85. **Mark:** i.e., listen to

86. **compromised:** agreed

87. **eanlings:** lambs; **pied:** particolored

88. **fall as Jacob's hire:** become Jacob's wages; **rank:** i.e., in heat

92. **pilled me:** peeled (The **me** is the ethical dative, which serves only to mark Shylock's speech as informal.)

94. **fulsome:** lustful

95. **eaning:** lambing

96. **Fall:** i.e., drop, give birth to

98. **thrift:** profit

99–101. **This was a venture . . . hand of heaven:** Antonio argues that Jacob was like a merchant venturing for profit with heaven's aid rather than (as Shylock had suggested) a usurer breeding interest.

102. **Was this . . . good?:** i.e., was the story of Jacob and Laban brought in to justify taking interest?

(As his wise mother wrought in his behalf)
The third possessor; ay, he was the third—

ANTONIO
And what of him? Did he take interest?

SHYLOCK
No, not take interest, not, as you would say,
Directly "interest." Mark what Jacob did.   85
When Laban and himself were compromised
That all the eanlings which were streaked and pied
Should fall as Jacob's hire, the ewes being rank
In end of autumn turnèd to the rams,
And when the work of generation was   90
Between these woolly breeders in the act,
The skillful shepherd pilled me certain wands,
And in the doing of the deed of kind
He stuck them up before the fulsome ewes,
Who then conceiving did in eaning time   95
Fall parti-colored lambs, and those were Jacob's.
This was a way to thrive, and he was blest;
And thrift is blessing if men steal it not.

ANTONIO
This was a venture, sir, that Jacob served for,
A thing not in his power to bring to pass,   100
But swayed and fashioned by the hand of heaven.
Was this inserted to make interest good?
Or is your gold and silver ewes and rams?

SHYLOCK
I cannot tell; I make it breed as fast.
But note me, signior—   105

ANTONIO, ⌈*aside to Bassanio*⌉
                    Mark you this, Bassanio,
The devil can cite Scripture for his purpose!
An evil soul producing holy witness
Is like a villain with a smiling cheek,
A goodly apple rotten at the heart.   110
O, what a goodly outside falsehood hath!

114. **rate:** i.e., rate of interest
115. **beholding to you:** i.e., in your debt
117. **rated:** berated, scolded
118. **moneys:** i.e., money, sums of money
119. **Still:** always
120. **suff'rance:** (1) forbearance; (2) suffering
122. **spet:** spit or spat; **gaberdine:** loose outer robe
123. **use:** (1) lending with interest; (2) using
125. **Go to:** an expression of impatience
127. **void your rheum:** i.e., spit
128. **foot:** i.e., kick
129. **suit:** i.e., what you seek
133. **bondman's key:** slave's tone of voice

Iudæus mercator patauinus

A Jewish merchant.
From Pietro Bertelli, *Diuersarum nationum
habitus . . .* (1594–96).

SHYLOCK
Three thousand ducats. 'Tis a good round sum.
Three months from twelve, then let me see, the
  rate—
ANTONIO
Well, Shylock, shall we be beholding to you?   115
SHYLOCK
Signior Antonio, many a time and oft
In the Rialto you have rated me
About my moneys and my usances.
Still have I borne it with a patient shrug
(For suff'rance is the badge of all our tribe).   120
You call me misbeliever, cutthroat dog,
And spet upon my Jewish gaberdine,
And all for use of that which is mine own.
Well then, it now appears you need my help.
Go to, then. You come to me and you say   125
"Shylock, we would have moneys"—you say so,
You, that did void your rheum upon my beard,
And foot me as you spurn a stranger cur
Over your threshold. Moneys is your suit.
What should I say to you? Should I not say   130
"Hath a dog money? Is it possible
A cur can lend three thousand ducats?" Or
Shall I bend low, and in a bondman's key,
With bated breath and whisp'ring humbleness,
Say this: "Fair sir, you spet on me on Wednesday   135
  last;
You spurned me such a day; another time
You called me 'dog'; and for these courtesies
I'll lend you thus much moneys"?
ANTONIO
I am as like to call thee so again,   140
To spet on thee again, to spurn thee, too.
If thou wilt lend this money, lend it not
As to thy friends, for when did friendship take

144. **breed . . . metal:** i.e., offspring (interest) for money (**metal**), which cannot breed naturally because it is infertile (**barren**)

146. **Who:** i.e., from whom; **break:** i.e., becomes bankrupt

151. **wants:** needs; **doit:** jot

154. **were:** i.e., would be (if it were done)

157. **single bond:** meaning uncertain

161. **nominated for:** named as; **equal:** exact

164. **Content:** agreed

167. **dwell:** remain; **necessity:** neediness

173. **teaches . . . suspect:** teach them to suspect

175. **break his day:** i.e., fail to repay me on the appointed day

A breed for barren metal of his friend?
But lend it rather to thine enemy,   145
Who, if he break, thou mayst with better face
Exact the penalty.
SHYLOCK   Why, look you how you storm!
I would be friends with you and have your love,
Forget the shames that you have stained me with,   150
Supply your present wants, and take no doit
Of usance for my moneys, and you'll not hear me!
This is kind I offer.
BASSANIO   This were kindness!
SHYLOCK   This kindness will I show.   155
Go with me to a notary, seal me there
Your single bond; and in a merry sport,
If you repay me not on such a day,
In such a place, such sum or sums as are
Expressed in the condition, let the forfeit   160
Be nominated for an equal pound
Of your fair flesh, to be cut off and taken
In what part of your body pleaseth me.
ANTONIO
Content, in faith. I'll seal to such a bond,
And say there is much kindness in the Jew.   165
BASSANIO
You shall not seal to such a bond for me!
I'll rather dwell in my necessity.
ANTONIO
Why, fear not, man, I will not forfeit it!
Within these two months—that's a month before
This bond expires—I do expect return   170
Of thrice three times the value of this bond.
SHYLOCK
O father Abram, what these Christians are,
Whose own hard dealings teaches them suspect
The thoughts of others! Pray you tell me this:
If he should break his day, what should I gain   175

178. **estimable:** valuable
181. **so:** i.e., fine
187. **fearful:** unreliable
188. **unthrifty knave:** careless servant
190. **Hie thee:** i.e., hurry

By the exaction of the forfeiture?
A pound of man's flesh taken from a man
Is not so estimable, profitable neither,
As flesh of muttons, beefs, or goats. I say,
To buy his favor I extend this friendship.   180
If he will take it, so. If not, adieu;
And for my love I pray you wrong me not.

ANTONIO
Yes, Shylock, I will seal unto this bond.

SHYLOCK
Then meet me forthwith at the notary's.
Give him direction for this merry bond,   185
And I will go and purse the ducats straight,
See to my house left in the fearful guard
Of an unthrifty knave, and presently
I'll be with you.

ANTONIO   Hie thee, gentle Jew.   190

⌈*Shylock*⌉ *exits.*

The Hebrew will turn Christian; he grows kind.

BASSANIO
I like not fair terms and a villain's mind.

ANTONIO
Come on, in this there can be no dismay;
My ships come home a month before the day.

They exit.

THE
MERCHANT
OF
VENICE

ACT 2

2.1 At Belmont the Prince of Morocco greets Portia, who tells him the terms of the contest: if he chooses the wrong chest, he must never again seek to marry. He accepts these terms.

———————

0 SD. **tawny:** brown; **accordingly:** i.e., costumed and made up in the same way as Morocco

1. **Mislike me not:** do not dislike me

2. **shadowed livery:** dark uniform

3. **near bred:** (1) brought up close by; (2) closely related

5. **Phoebus:** the god of the sun (See page 174.)

6. **make incision:** a surgical term

7. **reddest:** Red blood signified courage.

9. **feared:** terrified

14. **nice direction:** (1) precise guidance; (2) fastidious choice

15. **lott'ry of my destiny:** i.e., the test that will determine Portia's fate

17. **scanted:** restricted

18. **hedged . . . wit:** bound me through his wisdom

19. **who:** to whoever

⌈ACT 2⌉

⌈Scene 1⌉

*Enter ⌈the Prince of⌉ Morocco, a tawny Moor all in
white, and three or four followers accordingly, with
Portia, Nerissa, and their train.*

MOROCCO
Mislike me not for my complexion,
The shadowed livery of the burnished sun,
To whom I am a neighbor and near bred.
Bring me the fairest creature northward born,
Where Phoebus' fire scarce thaws the icicles,   5
And let us make incision for your love
To prove whose blood is reddest, his or mine.
I tell thee, lady, this aspect of mine
Hath feared the valiant; by my love I swear
The best regarded virgins of our clime   10
Have loved it too. I would not change this hue
Except to steal your thoughts, my gentle queen.

PORTIA
In terms of choice I am not solely led
By nice direction of a maiden's eyes;
Besides, the lott'ry of my destiny   15
Bars me the right of voluntary choosing.
But if my father had not scanted me
And hedged me by his wit to yield myself
His wife who wins me by that means I told you,

43

20. **stood as fair:** i.e., (1) looked as fair to me; (2) had as good a chance

26. **Sophy:** Persian ruler

27. **three fields:** i.e., three times on the battlefield; **Sultan Solyman:** i.e., Suleiman the Magnificent (See page 128.)

28. **o'erstare:** i.e., outstare

33. **Hercules and Lychas:** Hercules, the greatest of Greek mythological heroes, and his servant Lychas

34. **Which:** i.e., to determine which; **greater:** i.e., higher in points

36. **Alcides:** Hercules

44. **be advised:** take careful thought

45. **Nor will not:** i.e., I will not ever propose marriage to anyone, if I choose wrongly

"Blind Fortune." (2.1.37)
From Guillaume de la Perrière, *Le théâtre
des bons engins . . .* (1539).

Yourself, renownèd prince, then stood as fair   20
  As any comer I have looked on yet
  For my affection.
MOROCCO   Even for that I thank you.
  Therefore I pray you lead me to the caskets
  To try my fortune. By this scimitar   25
  That slew the Sophy and a Persian prince,
  That won three fields of Sultan Solyman,
  I would o'erstare the sternest eyes that look,
  Outbrave the heart most daring on the earth,
  Pluck the young sucking cubs from the she-bear,   30
  Yea, mock the lion when he roars for prey,
  To win ⌈thee,⌉ lady. But, alas the while!
  If Hercules and Lychas play at dice
  Which is the better man, the greater throw
  May turn by fortune from the weaker hand;   35
  So is Alcides beaten by his ⌈page,⌉
  And so may I, blind Fortune leading me,
  Miss that which one unworthier may attain,
  And die with grieving.
PORTIA   You must take your chance   40
  And either not attempt to choose at all
  Or swear before you choose, if you choose wrong
  Never to speak to lady afterward
  In way of marriage. Therefore be advised.
MOROCCO
  Nor will not. Come, bring me unto my chance.   45
PORTIA
  First, forward to the temple. After dinner
  Your hazard shall be made.
MOROCCO   Good fortune then,
  To make me blest—or cursed'st among men!
                                        They exit.

2.2 In Venice Shylock's servant, Lancelet Gobbo, debates whether he should find a new master. Lancelet's father comes in search of him and asks Bassanio to take Lancelet into his service. Bassanio agrees to become Lancelet's master. Bassanio also agrees to allow Gratiano to accompany him to Belmont, provided that Gratiano behave properly in public.

———————

0 SD. Lancelet. Editors almost always change this name to "Lancelot," but it appears as "Lancelet" or "Launcelet" throughout the First Quarto and the First Folio. Since "lancelet" was a word, meaning "lancet" or "small lance" (a small weapon or man-at-arms), we see no reason to change the name.

1–31. Certainly . . . run: Lancelet imagines himself the hero of a morality play, urged by "the fiend" to break his contract and run away from his master, and warned by his conscience that this would be dishonest and dishonorable.

10. courageous: eager; **pack:** i.e., leave; **Fia:** i.e., *via* (Italian for "away")

13–14. neck . . . heart: a comic personification in which the conscience hangs on the heart's neck

17–18. smack . . . taste: suggestive of sexual appetite

23. God bless the mark: a mild oath

25. saving . . . reverence: i.e., begging your pardon

27. incarnation: i.e., incarnate (Having characters ignorantly use the wrong word is a form of humor now called "malapropism"; it occurs frequently in Lancelet's speeches.)

⌜Scene 2⌝
Enter ⌜*Lancelet Gobbo*⌝ *the Clown, alone.*

LANCELET   Certainly my conscience will serve me to
run from this Jew my master. The fiend is at mine
elbow and tempts me, saying to me "Gobbo,
Lancelet Gobbo, good Lancelet," or "good Gobbo," or "good Lancelet Gobbo, use your legs, take   5
the start, run away." My conscience says "No. Take
heed, honest Lancelet, take heed, honest Gobbo,"
or, as aforesaid, "honest Lancelet Gobbo, do not
run; scorn running with thy heels." Well, the most
courageous fiend bids me pack. "Fia!" says the   10
fiend. "Away!" says the fiend. "For the heavens,
rouse up a brave mind," says the fiend, "and run!"
Well, my conscience, hanging about the neck of my
heart, says very wisely to me "My honest friend
Lancelet, being an honest man's son"—or rather,   15
an honest woman's son, for indeed my father did
something smack, something grow to—he had a
kind of taste—well, my conscience says "Lancelet,
budge not." "Budge," says the fiend. "Budge not,"
says my conscience. "Conscience," say I, "you   20
counsel well." "Fiend," say I, "you counsel well."
To be ruled by my conscience, I should stay with the
Jew my master, who (God bless the mark) is a kind
of devil; and to run away from the Jew, I should be
ruled by the fiend, who (saving your reverence) is   25
the devil himself. Certainly the Jew is the very devil
incarnation, and, in my conscience, my conscience
is but a kind of hard conscience to offer to counsel
me to stay with the Jew. The fiend gives the more
friendly counsel. I will run, fiend. My heels are at   30
your commandment. I will run.

Enter old Gobbo with a basket.

35. **sandblind:** half-blind

35–36. **high gravel-blind:** between half-blind (sandblind) and fully blind (stone blind)

36. **confusions:** i.e., conclusions (To "try conclusions" is to experiment.)

39–42. Possibly Lancelet turns his father around in a complete circle so that the father is facing the door to Shylock's house.

41. **marry:** i.e., indeed

42. **indirectly:** i.e., directly

43. **Be God's sonties:** by God's saints

46–63. **Master:** a term of respect usually reserved for gentlemen and thus inappropriate for Lancelet. Throughout this exchange, old Gobbo insists that his son is not "Master Lancelet" but simply "Lancelet," "a poor man's son."

47. **raise the waters:** perhaps, provoke his tears

51. **well to live:** likely to live a long time

54. **Your . . . sir:** a polite phrase to ask that a title not be used

55. **ergo:** Latin for "therefore"

57. **an 't:** i.e., if it

59. **father:** a courteous form of address

60–61. **Fates . . . Sisters Three:** The Fates were three goddesses, Clotho, Lachesis, and Atropos; they supposedly controlled a person's span of life.

66–67. **hovel-post:** post supporting a shed

GOBBO Master young man, you, I pray you, which is
the way to Master Jew's?

LANCELET, ⌈*aside*⌉ O heavens, this is my true begotten
father, who being more than sandblind, high gravel-   35
blind, knows me not. I will try confusions with him.

GOBBO Master young gentleman, I pray you, which is
the way to Master Jew's?

LANCELET Turn up on your right hand at the next
turning, but at the next turning of all on your left;   40
marry, at the very next turning, turn of no hand,
but turn down indirectly to the Jew's house.

GOBBO Be God's sonties, 'twill be a hard way to hit.
Can you tell me whether one Lancelet, that dwells
with him, dwell with him or no?   45

LANCELET Talk you of young Master Lancelet? ⌈*Aside.*⌉
Mark me now, now will I raise the waters.—Talk
you of young Master Lancelet?

GOBBO No master, sir, but a poor man's son. His
father, though I say 't, is an honest exceeding poor   50
man and, God be thanked, well to live.

LANCELET Well, let his father be what he will, we talk
of young Master Lancelet.

GOBBO Your Worship's friend, and Lancelet, sir.

LANCELET But I pray you, *ergo*, old man, *ergo*, I be-   55
seech you, talk you of young Master Lancelet?

GOBBO Of Lancelet, an 't please your mastership.

LANCELET *Ergo*, Master Lancelet. Talk not of Master
Lancelet, father, for the young gentleman, according to Fates and Destinies, and such odd sayings, the   60
Sisters Three, and such branches of learning, is
indeed deceased, or, as you would say in plain
terms, gone to heaven.

GOBBO Marry, God forbid! The boy was the very staff
of my age, my very prop.   65

LANCELET, ⌈*aside*⌉ Do I look like a cudgel or a hovel-
post, a staff or a prop?—Do you know me, father?

74–75. **It is . . . his own child:** inversion of the proverb "It is a wise child that knows his own father"

77–78. **Truth . . . hid long:** proverbs

88. **man:** servant

92. **Lord . . . be:** i.e., may the Lord be worshiped; **what a beard:** Onstage, the old man often grasps Lancelet's long hair as Lancelet faces away from him.

94. **fill-horse:** a horse that pulls between shafts

97. **hair of:** i.e., hair in; **have of:** i.e., have on

103. **set up my rest:** i.e., decided

"The Sisters Three." (2.2.61)
From Vincenzo Cartari, *Imagines deorum . . .* (1581).

GOBBO Alack the day, I know you not, young gentleman. But I pray you tell me, is my boy, God rest his
soul, alive or dead?   70
LANCELET Do you not know me, father?
GOBBO Alack, sir, I am sandblind. I know you not.
LANCELET Nay, indeed, if you had your eyes, you might
fail of the knowing me. It is a wise father that
knows his own child. Well, old man, I will tell you   75
news of your son. ⌜*He kneels.*⌝ Give me your blessing. Truth will come to light, murder cannot be hid
long—a man's son may, but in the end, truth will
out.
GOBBO Pray you, sir, stand up! I am sure you are not   80
Lancelet my boy.
LANCELET Pray you, let's have no more fooling about
it, but give me your blessing. I am Lancelet, your
boy that was, your son that is, your child that shall
be.   85
GOBBO I cannot think you are my son.
LANCELET I know not what I shall think of that; but I
am Lancelet, the Jew's man, and I am sure Margery
your wife is my mother.
GOBBO Her name is Margery, indeed. I'll be sworn if   90
thou be Lancelet, thou art mine own flesh and
blood. Lord worshiped might He be, what a beard
hast thou got! Thou hast got more hair on thy chin
than Dobbin my fill-horse has on his tail.
LANCELET, ⌜*standing up*⌝ It should seem, then, that   95
Dobbin's tail grows backward. I am sure he had
more hair of his tail than I have of my face when I
⌜last⌝ saw him.
GOBBO Lord, how art thou changed! How dost thou
and thy master agree? I have brought him a present. 100
How 'gree you now?
LANCELET Well, well. But for mine own part, as I have
set up my rest to run away, so I will not rest till I

105. **halter:** noose to hang him
106. **tell:** count
108. **Give me:** i.e., give
109. **liveries:** uniforms
115–16. **put . . . making:** i.e., get the uniforms made
117. **anon:** right now
120. **Gramercy:** thank you; **aught:** i.e., anything
124. **infection:** i.e., affection, desire
128–29. **saving your Worship's reverence:** i.e., begging your Lordship's pardon
129. **scarce cater-cousins:** hardly good friends
132. **frutify:** i.e., fructify (malapropism for, perhaps, notify)
136. **impertinent:** i.e., pertinent

have run some ground. My master's a very Jew.
Give him a present! Give him a halter. I am   105
famished in his service. You may tell every finger I
have with my ribs. Father, I am glad you are come!
Give me your present to one Master Bassanio, who
indeed gives rare new liveries. If I serve not him, I
will run as far as God has any ground. O rare   110
fortune, here comes the man! To him, father, for I
am a Jew if I serve the Jew any longer.

Enter Bassanio with ⌐Leonardo and⌐ a follower or two.

BASSANIO, ⌐*to an Attendant*⌐   You may do so, but let it be
so hasted that supper be ready at the farthest by five
of the clock. See these letters delivered, put the   115
liveries to making, and desire Gratiano to come
anon to my lodging.   ⌐*The Attendant exits.*⌐
LANCELET   To him, father.
GOBBO, ⌐*to Bassanio*⌐   God bless your Worship.
BASSANIO   Gramercy. Wouldst thou aught with me?   120
GOBBO   Here's my son, sir, a poor boy—
LANCELET   Not a poor boy, sir, but the rich Jew's man,
that would, sir, as my father shall specify—
GOBBO   He hath a great infection, sir, as one would say,
to serve—   125
LANCELET   Indeed, the short and the long is, I serve the
Jew, and have a desire, as my father shall specify—
GOBBO   His master and he (saving your Worship's
reverence) are scarce cater-cousins—
LANCELET   To be brief, the very truth is that the Jew,   130
having done me wrong, doth cause me, as my
father being, I hope, an old man, shall frutify unto
you—
GOBBO   I have here a dish of doves that I would bestow
upon your Worship, and my suit is—   135
LANCELET   In very brief, the suit is impertinent to
myself, as your Worship shall know by this honest

142. **defect:** i.e., perhaps, effect or purpose

145. **preferred:** i.e., recommended; **preferment:** advancement

148. **old proverb:** namely, "The grace of God is enough"; **parted:** divided

154. **guarded:** braided

155. **service:** position as a servant

157. **table:** palm of the hand

159. **go to:** expression of impatience; **line of life:** life-line (Lancelet begins reading his palm.)

161–62. **simple coming-in:** humble beginning

163–64. **to . . . featherbed:** a reference perhaps to the danger of marriage or of a sexual encounter

165. **for this gear:** for this business

167. **twinkling:** instant (twinkling of an eye)

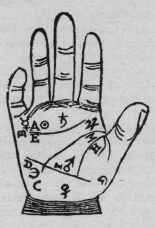

The "table" of the hand. (2.2.157)
From Joannes ab Indagine, *The book of palmestry . . .* (1666).

old man, and though I say it, though old man yet
poor man, my father—

BASSANIO   One speak for both. What would you?   140
LANCELET   Serve you, sir.
GOBBO   That is the very defect of the matter, sir.
BASSANIO, ⌜*to Lancelet*⌝
  I know thee well. Thou hast obtained thy suit.
  Shylock thy master spoke with me this day,
  And hath preferred thee, if it be preferment   145
  To leave a rich Jew's service, to become
  The follower of so poor a gentleman.
LANCELET   The old proverb is very well parted between
    my master Shylock and you, sir: you have "the
    grace of God," sir, and he hath "enough."   150
BASSANIO
  Thou speak'st it well.—Go, father, with thy son.—
  Take leave of thy old master, and inquire
  My lodging out. ⌜*To an Attendant.*⌝ Give him a livery
  More guarded than his fellows'. See it done.
                ⌜*Bassanio and his Attendants talk apart.*⌝
LANCELET   Father, in. I cannot get a service, no! I have   155
    ne'er a tongue in my head! Well, ⌜*studying his palm*⌝
    if any man in Italy have a fairer table which doth
    offer to swear upon a book—I shall have good
    fortune, go to! Here's a simple line of life. Here's a
    small trifle of wives—alas, fifteen wives is nothing;   160
    eleven widows and nine maids is a simple coming-
    in for one man—and then to 'scape drowning
    thrice, and to be in peril of my life with the edge of a
    featherbed! Here are simple 'scapes. Well, if For-
    tune be a woman, she's a good wench for this gear.   165
    Father, come. I'll take my leave of the Jew in the
    twinkling.   ⌜*Lancelet and old Gobbo*⌝ *exit.*
BASSANIO
  I pray thee, good Leonardo, think on this.
                          ⌜*Handing him a paper.*⌝

177. **suit to:** i.e., a request to make of

183. **Parts:** i.e., qualities; **happily:** agreeably

186–87. **show . . . liberal:** appear somewhat too free and easy

188. **allay:** moderate; **modesty:** self-control

190. **misconstered:** misunderstood

193. **put . . . habit:** i.e., assume a serious manner (literally, dress in dark clothes)

196. **saying:** i.e., being said

198. **Use . . . civility:** pay attention to manners

199. **sad ostent:** serious appearance

These things being bought and orderly bestowed,
Return in haste, for I do feast tonight   170
My best esteemed acquaintance. Hie thee, go.
LEONARDO
My best endeavors shall be done herein.

Enter Gratiano.

GRATIANO, ⌜*to Leonardo*⌝ Where's your master?
LEONARDO   Yonder, sir, he walks.   *Leonardo exits.*
GRATIANO   Signior Bassanio!   175
BASSANIO   Gratiano!
GRATIANO   I have suit to you.
BASSANIO   You have obtained it.
GRATIANO   You must not deny me. I must go with you
    to Belmont.   180
BASSANIO
Why then you must. But hear thee, Gratiano,
Thou art too wild, too rude and bold of voice—
Parts that become thee happily enough,
And in such eyes as ours appear not faults.
But where thou art not known—why, there they   185
    show
Something too liberal. Pray thee take pain
To allay with some cold drops of modesty
Thy skipping spirit, lest through thy wild behavior
I be misconstered in the place I go to,   190
And lose my hopes.
GRATIANO   Signior Bassanio, hear me.
If I do not put on a sober habit,
Talk with respect, and swear but now and then,
Wear prayer books in my pocket, look demurely,   195
Nay more, while grace is saying, hood mine eyes
Thus with my hat, and sigh and say "amen,"
Use all the observance of civility
Like one well studied in a sad ostent
To please his grandam, never trust me more.   200

202. **bar:** exclude (from my promise of good behavior)
204. **were pity:** would be a pity
207. **purpose:** intend

2.3 Jessica, Shylock's daughter, says good-bye to Lancelet and gives him a letter for Lorenzo, a friend of Bassanio. In a soliloquy, Jessica reveals her desire to marry Lorenzo.

---

10. **exhibit:** i.e., inhibit (malapropism)

BASSANIO   Well, we shall see your bearing.

GRATIANO
Nay, but I bar tonight. You shall not gauge me
By what we do tonight.

BASSANIO   No, that were pity.
I would entreat you rather to put on   205
Your boldest suit of mirth, for we have friends
That purpose merriment. But fare you well.
I have some business.

GRATIANO
And I must to Lorenzo and the rest.
But we will visit you at supper time.   210

They exit.

⌈Scene 3⌉
Enter Jessica and ⌈*Lancelet Gobbo.*⌉

JESSICA
I am sorry thou wilt leave my father so.
Our house is hell and thou, a merry devil,
Didst rob it of some taste of tediousness.
But fare thee well. There is a ducat for thee,
And, Lancelet, soon at supper shalt thou see   5
Lorenzo, who is thy new master's guest.
Give him this letter, do it secretly,
And so farewell. I would not have my father
See me in talk with thee.

LANCELET   Adieu. Tears exhibit my tongue, most beau-   10
tiful pagan, most sweet Jew. If a Christian do not
play the knave and get thee, I am much deceived.
But adieu. These foolish drops do something drown
my manly spirit. Adieu.

JESSICA   Farewell, good Lancelet.   15

⌈*Lancelet exits.*⌉

2.4 Lorenzo, Gratiano, Solanio, and Salarino try to arrange a masque for Bassanio's dinner that night. Lancelet brings Lorenzo Jessica's letter indicating that she will rob her father and, in disguise as a page, elope that night with Lorenzo.

———————

1. **in:** i.e., during
5. **spoke . . . of:** i.e., arranged to have
6. **it:** the **masque** that the gentlemen are planning (A masque was an impromptu masquerade. The performers wore masks and fancy clothing.); **quaintly ordered:** elegantly managed
7. **in my mind:** i.e., I think
9. **furnish us:** prepare ourselves

Masquers.
From Giacomo Franco, *Habiti d'huomeni* . . . (1609?).

Alack, what heinous sin is it in me
To be ashamed to be my father's child?
But though I am a daughter to his blood,
I am not to his manners. O Lorenzo,
If thou keep promise, I shall end this strife,   20
Become a Christian and thy loving wife.

She exits.

⌈Scene 4⌉
Enter Gratiano, Lorenzo, Salarino, and Solanio.

LORENZO
Nay, we will slink away in supper time,
Disguise us at my lodging, and return
All in an hour.
GRATIANO
We have not made good preparation.
SALARINO
We have not spoke us yet of torchbearers.   5
SOLANIO
'Tis vile, unless it may be quaintly ordered,
And better in my mind not undertook.
LORENZO
'Tis now but four o'clock. We have two hours
To furnish us.

Enter Lancelet.

　　　　　　　Friend Lancelet, what's the news?   10
LANCELET An it shall please you to break up this, it
　　shall seem to signify. *⌈Handing him Jessica's letter.⌉*
LORENZO
I know the hand; in faith, 'tis a fair hand,
And whiter than the paper it writ on
Is the fair hand that writ.   15
GRATIANO　　　　　　　Love news, in faith!

17. **By your leave, sir:** a polite indication that Lancelet would like permission to leave

27. **straight:** straightway, immediately

30. **some hour hence:** about an hour from now

39. **foot:** i.e., path

40. **she:** i.e., misfortune

41. **she:** Jessica

LANCELET   By your leave, sir.
LORENZO   Whither goest thou?
LANCELET   Marry, sir, to bid my old master the Jew to
   sup tonight with my new master the Christian.   20
LORENZO
   Hold here, take this. ⌐*Giving him money.*⌐ Tell gentle
     Jessica
   I will not fail her. Speak it privately.
                         ⌐*Lancelet*⌐ *exits.*

   Go, gentlemen,
   Will you prepare you for this masque tonight?   25
   I am provided of a torchbearer.
SALARINO
   Ay, marry, I'll be gone about it straight.
SOLANIO
   And so will I.
LORENZO   Meet me and Gratiano
   At Gratiano's lodging some hour hence.   30
SALARINO   'Tis good we do so.
              ⌐*Salarino and Solanio*⌐ *exit.*

GRATIANO
   Was not that letter from fair Jessica?
LORENZO
   I must needs tell thee all. She hath directed
   How I shall take her from her father's house,
   What gold and jewels she is furnished with,   35
   What page's suit she hath in readiness.
   If e'er the Jew her father come to heaven,
   It will be for his gentle daughter's sake;
   And never dare misfortune cross her foot
   Unless she do it under this excuse,   40
   That she is issue to a faithless Jew.
   Come, go with me. Peruse this as thou goest;
               ⌐*Handing him the letter.*⌐
   Fair Jessica shall be my torchbearer.
                    ⌐*They*⌐ *exit.*

2.5 Lancelet brings Shylock an invitation to dinner at Bassanio's. Shylock grudgingly accepts and commands Jessica to guard their house carefully. Lancelet also manages to tell Jessica that Lorenzo is coming for her that night.

———————

2. **of:** i.e., between
3. **What:** an interjection
5. **rend apparel out:** i.e., wear out clothes
8. **bids thee call:** asked you to call
13. **wherefore:** why
14. **bid for love:** i.e., invited because of affection
17. **right:** very
18. **rest:** i.e., peace of mind
19. **tonight:** i.e., last night
21. **reproach:** i.e., approach (Shylock takes the word literally.)
25. **nose fell a-bleeding:** supposed an evil omen
25–28. **on Black Monday . . . afternoon:** This is a parody of prognostication. **Black Monday:** Easter Monday

⌜Scene 5⌝
Enter ⌜*Shylock, the*⌝ *Jew, and* ⌜*Lancelet,*⌝
his man that was, the Clown.

SHYLOCK
Well, thou shalt see, thy eyes shall be thy judge,
The difference of old Shylock and Bassanio.—
What, Jessica!—Thou shalt not gormandize
As thou hast done with me—what, Jessica!—
And sleep, and snore, and rend apparel out.—   5
Why, Jessica, I say!

LANCELET   Why, Jessica!

SHYLOCK
Who bids thee call? I do not bid thee call.

LANCELET Your Worship was wont to tell me I could
do nothing without bidding.   10

Enter Jessica.

JESSICA Call you? What is your will?

SHYLOCK
I am bid forth to supper, Jessica.
There are my keys.—But wherefore should I go?
I am not bid for love. They flatter me.
But yet I'll go in hate, to feed upon   15
The prodigal Christian.—Jessica, my girl,
Look to my house.—I am right loath to go.
There is some ill a-brewing towards my rest,
For I did dream of money bags tonight.

LANCELET I beseech you, sir, go. My young master   20
doth expect your reproach.

SHYLOCK So do I his.

LANCELET And they have conspired together—I will
not say you shall see a masque, but if you do, then it
was not for nothing that my nose fell a-bleeding on   25
Black Monday last, at six o'clock i' th' morning,
falling out that year on Ash Wednesday was four
year in th' afternoon.

34. **varnished faces:** i.e., painted masks

36. **fopp'ry:** foolishness

37. **Jacob:** wealthy patriarch in the Old Testament

38. **of feasting:** i.e., to feast

42. **for all this:** i.e., in spite of what Shylock has said

45. **fool . . . offspring:** gentile outcast (Abraham's son by Hagar, a gentile, was the outcast Ishmael.)

47. **patch:** i.e., fool

48. **in profit:** i.e., in doing anything that pays

49. **Drones hive not with me:** i.e., bees that do not work can't stay in my hive

55. **Fast bind, fast find:** a proverb that seems to mean "If you secure something tightly, you'll return to find it tightly secured"

"Varnished faces." (2.5.34)
From Guillaume de la Perrière, *Le théâtre des bons engins . . .* (1539).

SHYLOCK
What, are there masques? Hear you me, Jessica,
Lock up my doors, and when you hear the drum   30
And the vile squealing of the wry-necked fife,
Clamber not you up to the casements then,
Nor thrust your head into the public street
To gaze on Christian fools with varnished faces,
But stop my house's ears (I mean my casements).   35
Let not the sound of shallow fopp'ry enter
My sober house. By Jacob's staff I swear
I have no mind of feasting forth tonight.
But I will go.—Go you before me, sirrah.
Say I will come.   40
LANCELET   I will go before, sir. ⌜*Aside to Jessica.*⌝ Mis-
    tress, look out at window for all this.
There will come a Christian by
Will be worth a ⌜'Jewess'⌝ eye.   ⌜*He exits.*⌝
SHYLOCK
What says that fool of Hagar's offspring, ha?   45
JESSICA
His words were "Farewell, mistress," nothing else.
SHYLOCK
The patch is kind enough, but a huge feeder,
Snail-slow in profit, and he sleeps by day
More than the wildcat. Drones hive not with me,
Therefore I part with him, and part with him   50
To one that I would have him help to waste
His borrowed purse. Well, Jessica, go in.
Perhaps I will return immediately.
Do as I bid you. Shut doors after you.
Fast bind, fast find—   55
A proverb never stale in thrifty mind.   *He exits.*
JESSICA
Farewell, and if my fortune be not crossed,
I have a father, you a daughter, lost.
                                              She exits.

2.6 Gratiano and Salarino wait for Lorenzo near Shylock's house. As soon as Lorenzo arrives, he calls Jessica, who throws him down her father's treasures and goes off with him to be married. Antonio enters to announce that Bassanio is about to sail for Belmont.

———————

1. **penthouse:** overhanging roof
2. **make stand:** i.e., stand
6. **Venus' pigeons:** irreverent reference to the doves that draw the chariot of the mythological goddess of love, Venus
8. **obligèd:** contracted
9. **ever holds:** is always true
11. **untread:** retrace
12. **measures:** paces
15. **younger:** i.e., younger son; **prodigal:** i.e., the prodigal son of Luke 15, who "wasted his substance"
16. **scarfèd:** adorned with flags and pennants
19. **overweathered:** weatherbeaten; **ribs:** timbers
22. **your patience:** i.e., please grant me your patience; **my long abode:** i.e., your long wait for me
26. **father:** i.e., father-in-law to be

⌜Scene 6⌝
Enter the masquers, Gratiano and Salarino.

GRATIANO
  This is the penthouse under which Lorenzo
  Desired us to make stand.
SALARINO   His hour is almost past.
GRATIANO
  And it is marvel he outdwells his hour,
  For lovers ever run before the clock.   5
SALARINO
  O, ten times faster Venus' pigeons fly
  To seal love's bonds new-made than they are wont
  To keep obligèd faith unforfeited.
GRATIANO
  That ever holds. Who riseth from a feast
  With that keen appetite that he sits down?   10
  Where is the horse that doth untread again
  His tedious measures with the unbated fire
  That he did pace them first? All things that are,
  Are with more spirit chasèd than enjoyed.
  How like a younger or a prodigal   15
  The scarfèd bark puts from her native bay,
  Hugged and embracèd by the strumpet wind;
  How like the prodigal doth she return
  With overweathered ribs and raggèd sails,
  Lean, rent, and beggared by the strumpet wind!   20

Enter Lorenzo.

SALARINO
  Here comes Lorenzo. More of this hereafter.
LORENZO
  Sweet friends, your patience for my long abode.
  Not I but my affairs have made you wait.
  When you shall please to play the thieves for wives,
  I'll watch as long for you then. Approach.   25
  Here dwells my father Jew.—Ho! Who's within?

28. **tongue:** i.e., sound of your voice

36. **exchange:** i.e., change, through disguise, from woman to boy

38. **pretty:** ingenious, clever, skillful

39. **Cupid:** Roman god of love

42. **hold a candle to:** i.e., illuminate

43. **good sooth:** i.e., in truth; **light:** (1) unrespectable; (2) illumined

44. **'tis an office of discovery:** i.e., the function of torchbearing is to bring to light, or discover

47. **garnish:** dress, costume

49. **close:** (1) dark; (2) secretive; **doth play the runaway:** i.e., passes quickly

"Love [Cupid] is blind." (2.6.37)
From Guillaume de la Perrière, *Le théâtre des bons engins . . .* (1539).

⌜*Enter*⌝ *Jessica above,* ⌜*dressed as a boy.*⌝

JESSICA
Who are you? Tell me for more certainty,
Albeit I'll swear that I do know your tongue.
LORENZO   Lorenzo, and thy love.
JESSICA
Lorenzo certain, and my love indeed,   30
For who love I so much? And now who knows
But you, Lorenzo, whether I am yours?
LORENZO
Heaven and thy thoughts are witness that thou art.
JESSICA
Here, catch this casket; it is worth the pains.
I am glad 'tis night, you do not look on me,   35
For I am much ashamed of my exchange.
But love is blind, and lovers cannot see
The pretty follies that themselves commit,
For if they could, Cupid himself would blush
To see me thus transformèd to a boy.   40
LORENZO
Descend, for you must be my torchbearer.
JESSICA
What, must I hold a candle to my shames?
They in themselves, good sooth, are too too light.
Why, 'tis an office of discovery, love,
And I should be obscured.   45
LORENZO   So are you, sweet,
Even in the lovely garnish of a boy.
But come at once,
For the close night doth play the runaway,
And we are stayed for at Bassanio's feast.   50
JESSICA
I will make fast the doors and gild myself
With some more ducats, and be with you straight.
                              ⌜*Jessica exits, above.*⌝

53. **by my hood:** a mild oath; **gentle:** i.e., gentile
54. **Beshrew me:** i.e., curse me (a mild oath); **but:** unless
60. **gentleman:** i.e., Jessica in disguise
67. **presently:** immediately
69. **on 't:** i.e., of it

2.7 At Belmont the Prince of Morocco attempts to choose the right chest and win Portia. He picks the gold one and finds in it a skull and a warning not to choose on the basis of appearances. He leaves in disappointment.

———————

1. **discover:** reveal

GRATIANO
  Now, by my hood, a gentle and no Jew!
LORENZO
  Beshrew me but I love her heartily,
  For she is wise, if I can judge of her,   55
  And fair she is, if that mine eyes be true,
  And true she is, as she hath proved herself.
  And therefore, like herself, wise, fair, and true,
  Shall she be placèd in my constant soul.

            Enter Jessica, ⌐*below.*¬

  What, art thou come? On, gentleman, away!   60
  Our masquing mates by this time for us stay.
                            ⌐*All but Gratiano*¬ *exit.*

            Enter Antonio.

ANTONIO   Who's there?
GRATIANO   Signior Antonio?
ANTONIO
  Fie, fie, Gratiano, where are all the rest?
  'Tis nine o' clock! Our friends all stay for you.   65
  No masque tonight; the wind is come about;
  Bassanio presently will go aboard.
  I have sent twenty out to seek for you.
GRATIANO
  I am glad on 't. I desire no more delight
  Than to be under sail and gone tonight.   70
                            They exit.

            ⌐*Scene 7*¬
Enter Portia with ⌐*the Prince of*¬ *Morocco and both their*
                trains.

PORTIA
  Go, draw aside the curtains and discover

2. **several:** various

10. **all as blunt:** i.e., as blunt (straightforward) as lead is blunt (dull)

15. **withal:** i.e., together with the picture

17. **back again:** i.e., again

24. **shows of dross:** appearances of worthlessness

25. **nor . . . nor:** neither . . . nor; **aught:** anything

26. **virgin hue:** Silver is the color of the moon, whose goddess, Diana, is patron of chastity.

31. **rated . . . estimation:** valued in accord with your reputation

The several caskets to this noble prince.
⌐*A curtain is drawn.*⌐
Now make your choice.

MOROCCO

This first, of gold, who this inscription bears,
"Who chooseth me shall gain what many men   5
  desire";
The second, silver, which this promise carries,
"Who chooseth me shall get as much as he
  deserves";
This third, dull lead, with warning all as blunt,   10
"Who chooseth me must give and hazard all he
  hath."
How shall I know if I do choose the right?

PORTIA

The one of them contains my picture, prince.
If you choose that, then I am yours withal.   15

MOROCCO

Some god direct my judgment! Let me see.
I will survey th' inscriptions back again.
What says this leaden casket?
"Who chooseth me must give and hazard all he
  hath."   20
Must give—for what? For lead? Hazard for lead?
This casket threatens. Men that hazard all
Do it in hope of fair advantages.
A golden mind stoops not to shows of dross.
I'll then nor give nor hazard aught for lead.   25
What says the silver with her virgin hue?
"Who chooseth me shall get as much as he
  deserves."
As much as he deserves—pause there, Morocco,
And weigh thy value with an even hand.   30
If thou beest rated by thy estimation,
Thou dost deserve enough; and yet enough
May not extend so far as to the lady.

34. **afeard . . . deserving:** afraid that I do not deserve

35. **Were:** i.e., would be; **disabling:** discrediting

47. **Hyrcanian deserts:** wild regions south of the Caspian Sea; **vasty:** i.e., vast

50. **watery kingdom:** i.e., the ocean

51. **Spets:** spits

52. **spirits:** i.e., persons

55. **like:** i.e., likely

57. **rib:** enclose; **cerecloth:** grave clothes

59. **Being . . . gold:** i.e., since silver is worth one tenth the value of proven gold

63. **insculped upon:** engraved on the surface

68. **form:** i.e., picture

And yet to be afeard of my deserving
Were but a weak disabling of myself.   35
As much as I deserve—why, that's the lady!
I do in birth deserve her, and in fortunes,
In graces, and in qualities of breeding,
But more than these, in love I do deserve.
What if I strayed no farther, but chose here?   40
Let's see once more this saying graved in gold:
"Who chooseth me shall gain what many men
    desire."
Why, that's the lady! All the world desires her.
From the four corners of the earth they come   45
To kiss this shrine, this mortal, breathing saint.
The Hyrcanian deserts and the vasty wilds
Of wide Arabia are as throughfares now
For princes to come view fair Portia.
The watery kingdom, whose ambitious head   50
Spets in the face of heaven, is no bar
To stop the foreign spirits, but they come
As o'er a brook to see fair Portia.
One of these three contains her heavenly picture.
Is 't like that lead contains her? 'Twere damnation   55
To think so base a thought. It were too gross
To rib her cerecloth in the obscure grave.
Or shall I think in silver she's immured,
Being ten times undervalued to tried gold?
O, sinful thought! Never so rich a gem   60
Was set in worse than gold. They have in England
A coin that bears the figure of an angel
Stamped in gold, but that's insculped upon;
But here an angel in a golden bed
Lies all within.—Deliver me the key.   65
Here do I choose, and thrive I as I may.

PORTIA
There, take it, prince. ⌈*Handing him the key.*⌉ And if
    my form lie there,
Then I am yours.

71. **carrion death:** i.e., a skull
73. **glisters:** glitters
76. **But:** only
80. **enscrolled:** i.e., on a scroll rather than in the person of Portia
83. **farewell, heat, and welcome frost:** an inversion of the saying "farewell, frost"
85. **part:** depart
87. **complexion:** (1) temperament; (2) color of the face

2.8 In Venice Solanio and Salarino discuss the latest news: Shylock's torment over the loss of his daughter and the treasures that she took; the destruction of an Italian ship in the English Channel; Antonio's sadness at the departure of Bassanio.

————————

⌜*Morocco opens the gold casket.*⌝
MOROCCO   O, hell! What have we here?   70
A carrion death within whose empty eye
There is a written scroll. I'll read the writing:
    All that glisters is not gold—
    Often have you heard that told.
    Many a man his life hath sold   75
    But my outside to behold.
    Gilded ⌜*tombs*⌝ *do worms infold.*
    Had you been as wise as bold,
    Young in limbs, in judgment old,
    Your answer had not been enscrolled.   80
    Fare you well, your suit is cold.
Cold indeed and labor lost!
Then, farewell, heat, and welcome frost.
Portia, adieu. I have too grieved a heart
To take a tedious leave. Thus losers part.   85
                He exits, ⌜*with his train.*⌝
PORTIA
A gentle riddance! Draw the curtains, go.
Let all of his complexion choose me so.
                        They exit.

⌜Scene 8⌝
Enter Salarino and Solanio.

SALARINO
Why, man, I saw Bassanio under sail;
With him is Gratiano gone along;
And in their ship I am sure Lorenzo is not.
SOLANIO
The villain Jew with outcries raised the Duke,
Who went with him to search Bassanio's ship.   5
SALARINO
He came too late; the ship was under sail.

12. **passion:** i.e., emotional outburst

20. **stones:** jewels (The word also meant "testicles.")

26. **look . . . day:** i.e., take care that he pay his loan on the appointed day

29. **reasoned:** spoke

30. **the Narrow Seas:** the English Channel

31. **miscarrièd:** was wrecked

32. **fraught:** freighted, loaded with goods

35. **You were best to:** i.e., you should

A gondola. (2.8.8)
From Cesare Vecellio, *Habiti antichi . . .* (1598).

But there the Duke was given to understand
That in a gondola were seen together
Lorenzo and his amorous Jessica.
Besides, Antonio certified the Duke   10
They were not with Bassanio in his ship.

SOLANIO
I never heard a passion so confused,
So strange, outrageous, and so variable
As the dog Jew did utter in the streets.
"My daughter, O my ducats, O my daughter!   15
Fled with a Christian! O my Christian ducats!
Justice, the law, my ducats, and my daughter,
A sealèd bag, two sealèd bags of ducats,
Of double ducats, stol'n from me by my daughter,
And jewels—two stones, two rich and precious   20
      stones—
Stol'n by my daughter! Justice! Find the girl!
She hath the stones upon her, and the ducats."

SALARINO
Why, all the boys in Venice follow him,
Crying "His stones, his daughter, and his ducats."   25

SOLANIO
Let good Antonio look he keep his day,
Or he shall pay for this.

SALARINO   Marry, well remembered.
I reasoned with a Frenchman yesterday
Who told me, in the Narrow Seas that part   30
The French and English, there miscarrièd
A vessel of our country richly fraught.
I thought upon Antonio when he told me,
And wished in silence that it were not his.

SOLANIO
You were best to tell Antonio what you hear—   35
Yet do not suddenly, for it may grieve him.

SALARINO
A kinder gentleman treads not the earth.

41. **Slubber not:** do not sloppily perform
42. **stay . . . riping:** await ripening or completion
43. **for:** i.e., as for
44. **mind of love:** i.e., love plans
46. **ostents:** appearances
50. **wondrous:** i.e., wondrously; **sensible:** (1) acutely felt; (2) strikingly evident
52. **he only . . . for him:** i.e., he loves the world only because Bassanio is in it
54. **quicken:** i.e., enliven; **embracèd heaviness:** i.e., the sorrow from which he voluntarily suffers

2.9 At Belmont the Prince of Arragon attempts to win Portia by choosing the silver chest, but finds in it the picture of a blinking idiot. He leaves. A messenger announces the arrival of a splendid envoy from another suitor. Nerissa prays that this one is Bassanio.

———————

0 SD. **Servitor:** servant
3. **to his election:** to make his choice (of casket)
5. **I:** i.e., my picture

I saw Bassanio and Antonio part.
Bassanio told him he would make some speed
Of his return. He answered "Do not so.   40
⌜Slubber⌝ not business for my sake, Bassanio,
But stay the very riping of the time;
And for the Jew's bond which he hath of me,
Let it not enter in your mind of love.
Be merry, and employ your chiefest thoughts   45
To courtship and such fair ostents of love
As shall conveniently become you there."
And even there, his eye being big with tears,
Turning his face, he put his hand behind him,
And with affection wondrous sensible   50
He wrung Bassanio's hand—and so they parted.

SOLANIO
I think he only loves the world for him.
I pray thee, let us go and find him out
And quicken his embracèd heaviness
With some delight or other.   55

SALARINO   Do we so.

They exit.

⌜Scene 9⌝
Enter Nerissa and a Servitor.

NERISSA
Quick, quick, I pray thee, draw the curtain straight.
The Prince of Arragon hath ta'en his oath
And comes to his election presently.

Enter ⌜the Prince of⌝ Arragon, his train, and Portia.

PORTIA
Behold, there stand the caskets, noble prince.
If you choose that wherein I am contained,   5
Straight shall our nuptial rites be solemnized.

12. **Of:** i.e., to choose
13. **in way of:** i.e., for the purpose of
14. **in fortune of:** i.e., to be fortunate in
18. **addressed me:** i.e., made myself ready; **Fortune:** i.e., good luck
26–28. **may be meant / By:** i.e., may mean
29. **fond:** foolish
30. **martlet:** house martin
31. **in:** exposed to
32. **Even . . . casualty:** i.e., directly in the way of powerfully destructive accident
34. **jump:** i.e., identify

But if you fail, without more speech, my lord,
You must be gone from hence immediately.

ARRAGON
I am enjoined by oath to observe three things:
First, never to unfold to anyone   10
Which casket 'twas I chose; next, if I fail
Of the right casket, never in my life
To woo a maid in way of marriage;
Lastly, if I do fail in fortune of my choice,
Immediately to leave you, and be gone.   15

PORTIA
To these injunctions everyone doth swear
That comes to hazard for my worthless self.

ARRAGON
And so have I addressed me. Fortune now
To my heart's hope! Gold, silver, and base lead.
"Who chooseth me must give and hazard all he   20
    hath."
You shall look fairer ere I give or hazard.
What says the golden chest? Ha, let me see:
"Who chooseth me shall gain what many men
    desire."   25
What many men desire—that "many" may be
    meant
By the fool multitude that choose by show,
Not learning more than the fond eye doth teach,
Which pries not to th' interior, but like the martlet 30
Builds in the weather on the outward wall,
Even in the force and road of casualty.
I will not choose what many men desire,
Because I will not jump with common spirits
And rank me with the barbarous multitudes.   35
Why, then, to thee, thou silver treasure house.
Tell me once more what title thou dost bear.
"Who chooseth me shall get as much as he
    deserves."

40. **go about:** set out
41. **cozen:** trick, deceive
44. **degrees:** rank
47. **should . . . bare:** i.e., should keep their hats on who now take them off in deference
49. **gleaned:** separated and discarded (as chaff from seed)
52. **new varnished:** i.e., newly restored to former status
55. **assume desert:** i.e., assume that I deserve the best
59. **schedule:** scroll

And well said, too; for who shall go about   40
To cozen fortune and be honorable
Without the stamp of merit? Let none presume
To wear an undeservèd dignity.
O, that estates, degrees, and offices
Were not derived corruptly, and that clear honor   45
Were purchased by the merit of the wearer!
How many then should cover that stand bare?
How many be commanded that command?
How much low peasantry would then be gleaned
From the true seed of honor? And how much honor   50
Picked from the chaff and ruin of the times,
To be new varnished? Well, but to my choice.
"Who chooseth me shall get as much as he
    deserves."
I will assume desert. Give me a key for this,   55
                              ⌜*He is given a key.*⌝
And instantly unlock my fortunes here.
                              ⌜*He opens the silver casket.*⌝
PORTIA
Too long a pause for that which you find there.
ARRAGON
What's here? The portrait of a blinking idiot
Presenting me a schedule! I will read it.—
How much unlike art thou to Portia!   60
How much unlike my hopes and my deservings.
"Who chooseth me shall have as much as he
    deserves"?
Did I deserve no more than a fool's head?
Is that my prize? Are my deserts no better?   65
PORTIA
To offend and judge are distinct offices
And of opposèd natures.
ARRAGON   What is here?
⌜*He reads.*⌝

69. **tried:** tested; **this:** (1) the silver casket; (2) the sayings that follow

72. **shadows:** images

74. **iwis:** certainly

75. **Silvered o'er:** (1) with gray hair; (2) adorned with or possessing silver

78. **sped:** ruined

80. **By the time:** i.e., the more time

84. **wroth:** (1) wrath, anger; (2) ruth, sorrow

86. **deliberate:** calculating, reasoning

97. **sensible regreets:** material greetings, i.e., gifts

98. **commends:** greetings; **breath:** i.e., words

99. **yet:** i.e., before now

"The candle singed the moth." (2.9.85)
From Filippo Picinelli, *Mundus symbolicus* . . . (1687).

> *The fire seven times tried this;*
> *Seven times tried that judgment is*   70
> *That did never choose amiss.*
> *Some there be that shadows kiss;*
> *Such have but a shadow's bliss.*
> *There be fools alive, iwis,*
> *Silvered o'er—and so was this.*   75
> *Take what wife you will to bed,*
> *I will ever be your head.*
> *So begone; you are sped.*

Still more fool I shall appear
By the time I linger here.   80
With one fool's head I came to woo,
But I go away with two.
Sweet, adieu. I'll keep my oath,
Patiently to bear my wroth. ⌜*He exits with his train.*⌝

PORTIA
Thus hath the candle singed the moth.   85
O, these deliberate fools, when they do choose,
They have the wisdom by their wit to lose.

NERISSA
The ancient saying is no heresy:
Hanging and wiving goes by destiny.

PORTIA   Come, draw the curtain, Nerissa.   90

Enter Messenger.

MESSENGER   Where is my lady?
PORTIA   Here. What would my
  lord?
MESSENGER
Madam, there is alighted at your gate
A young Venetian, one that comes before   95
To signify th' approaching of his lord,
From whom he bringeth sensible regrets;
To wit (besides commends and courteous breath),
Gifts of rich value; yet I have not seen

100. **likely:** (1) attractive; (2) promising

102. **costly:** lavish, rich

106. **high-day:** high holiday; i.e., extraordinary

108. **Cupid:** god of love; **post:** messenger; **mannerly:** courteously

109. **Bassanio . . . be!:** i.e., if it is your will, Cupid (Lord Love), let it be Bassanio (who has come, or who will win Portia)

So likely an ambassador of love. 100
A day in April never came so sweet,
To show how costly summer was at hand,
As this fore-spurrer comes before his lord.

PORTIA
No more, I pray thee. I am half afeard
Thou wilt say anon he is some kin to thee, 105
Thou spend'st such high-day wit in praising him!
Come, come, Nerissa, for I long to see
Quick Cupid's post that comes so mannerly.

NERISSA
Bassanio, Lord Love, if thy will it be!

They exit.

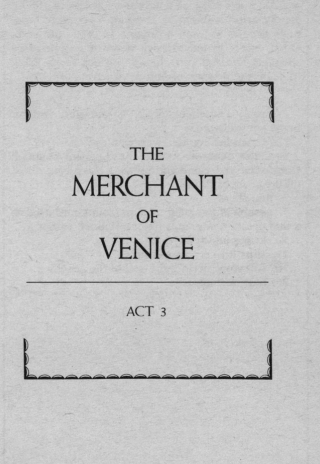

THE
MERCHANT
OF
VENICE

ACT 3

3.1   In Venice Solanio and Salarino have learned that the Italian ship wrecked in the English Channel was Antonio's. Shylock enters angry at Jessica's flight. He declares his intention of taking a pound of Antonio's flesh if Antonio is unable to repay the loan. Tubal enters to tell Shylock news of Jessica's free spending and Antonio's losses. Shylock sends Tubal to begin the process of Antonio's arrest.

---

2. **lives . . . unchecked:** i.e., is said there without being contradicted

3. **of rich lading:** i.e., with rich cargo

3–4. **the Narrow Seas:** the English Channel; **Goodwins:** the Goodwin Sands, a dangerous shoal off the coast of Kent

5. **flat:** shoal

7. **gossip:** a gossiping woman (sometimes used as a title before a woman's name); **Report:** rumor

10. **knapped:** nibbled

12. **slips of:** i.e., lapses into

16. **full stop:** period, the end of the sentence

20. **betimes:** quickly

⌜ACT 3⌝

⌜Scene 1⌝
⌜*Enter*⌝ *Solanio and Salarino.*

SOLANIO Now, what news on the Rialto?

SALARINO Why, yet it lives there unchecked that Antonio hath a ship of rich lading wracked on the
Narrow Seas—the Goodwins, I think they call the
place—a very dangerous flat, and fatal, where the   5
carcasses of many a tall ship lie buried, as they say,
if my gossip Report be an honest woman of her
word.

SOLANIO I would she were as lying a gossip in that as
ever knapped ginger or made her neighbors be-   10
lieve she wept for the death of a third husband. But
it is true, without any slips of prolixity or crossing
the plain highway of talk, that the good Antonio,
the honest Antonio—O, that I had a title good
enough to keep his name company!—   15

SALARINO Come, the full stop.

SOLANIO Ha, what sayest thou? Why, the end is, he
hath lost a ship.

SALARINO I would it might prove the end of his losses.

SOLANIO Let me say "amen" betimes, lest the devil   20
cross my prayer, for here he comes in the likeness
of a Jew.

Enter Shylock.

95

28. **withal:** i.e., with

30. **fledge:** ready to fly; **complexion:** nature

31. **dam:** mother

34. **flesh and blood:** i.e., child (The phrase can also mean one's sensual appetites, which is the way Solanio pretends to understand it.)

35. **Out upon it:** i.e., curse it; **carrion:** dead flesh

41. **Rhenish:** white wine from the Rhineland

43. **match:** bargain, deal

43–44. **bankrout:** i.e., bankrupt

46. **upon the mart:** to the place where merchants gather

46–47. **was wont to call:** used to call

47. **usurer:** moneylender, especially one who charges an excessive rate of interest, or "use" (See page 98.)

48. **for a . . . cur'sy:** i.e., as a . . . courtesy

52. **bait:** i.e., use as bait for

54. **hindered me:** i.e., kept me from making

56. **bargains:** i.e., deals

How now, Shylock, what news among the merchants?

SHYLOCK   You knew, none so well, none so well as you,   25
of my daughter's flight.

SALARINO   That's certain. I for my part knew the tailor
that made the wings she flew withal.

SOLANIO   And Shylock for his own part knew the bird
was fledge, and then it is the complexion of them   30
all to leave the dam.

SHYLOCK   She is damned for it.

SALARINO   That's certain, if the devil may be her judge.

SHYLOCK   My own flesh and blood to rebel!

SOLANIO   Out upon it, old carrion! Rebels it at these   35
years?

SHYLOCK   I say my daughter is my flesh and my blood.

SALARINO   There is more difference between thy flesh
and hers than between jet and ivory, more between
your bloods than there is between red wine and   40
Rhenish. But tell us, do you hear whether Antonio
have had any loss at sea or no?

SHYLOCK   There I have another bad match! A bankrout, a prodigal, who dare scarce show his head on
the Rialto, a beggar that was used to come so smug   45
upon the mart! Let him look to his bond. He was
wont to call me usurer; let him look to his bond. He
was wont to lend money for a Christian cur'sy; let
him look to his bond.

SALARINO   Why, I am sure if he forfeit, thou wilt not   50
take his flesh! What's that good for?

SHYLOCK   To bait fish withal; if it will feed nothing else,
it will feed my revenge. He hath disgraced me and
hindered me half a million, laughed at my losses,
mocked at my gains, scorned my nation, thwarted   55
my bargains, cooled my friends, heated mine ene-
mies—and what's his reason? I am a Jew. Hath not
a Jew eyes? Hath not a Jew hands, organs, dimen-

68. **his humility:** i.e., the Christian's kindness

69. **his sufferance:** i.e., the Jew's forbearance; **by:** according to

71–72. **it shall go hard but . . . instruction:** i.e., with any luck I will do better than my teacher

76. **another of the tribe:** i.e., another Jew

76–77. **a third cannot be matched:** i.e., there will never be a third person like these two

86. **that:** i.e., the diamond

89. **would:** i.e., I wish; **hearsed:** in her coffin

A usurer. (3.1.47)
From John Blaxton, *The English vsurer . . .* (1634).

sions, senses, affections, passions? Fed with the
same food, hurt with the same weapons, subject to   60
the same diseases, healed by the same means,
warmed and cooled by the same winter and summer as a Christian is? If you prick us, do we not
bleed? If you tickle us, do we not laugh? If you
poison us, do we not die? And if you wrong us, shall   65
we not revenge? If we are like you in the rest, we will
resemble you in that. If a Jew wrong a Christian,
what is his humility? Revenge. If a Christian wrong
a Jew, what should his sufferance be by Christian
example? Why, revenge! The villainy you teach me I   70
will execute, and it shall go hard but I will better the
instruction.

Enter a man from Antonio.

⌐SERVINGMAN⌐   Gentlemen, my master Antonio is at his
house and desires to speak with you both.
SALARINO   We have been up and down to seek him.   75

Enter Tubal.

SOLANIO   Here comes another of the tribe; a third
cannot be matched unless the devil himself turn
Jew.
⌐*Salarino, Solanio, and the Servingman*⌐ *exit.*
SHYLOCK   How now, Tubal, what news from Genoa?
Hast thou found my daughter?   80
TUBAL   I often came where I did hear of her, but
cannot find her.
SHYLOCK   Why, there, there, there, there! A diamond
gone cost me two thousand ducats in Frankfurt!
The curse never fell upon our nation till now, I   85
never felt it till now. Two thousand ducats in that,
and other precious, precious jewels! I would my
daughter were dead at my foot and the jewels in her
ear; would she were hearsed at my foot and the

94. **a' my:** i.e., on my

95, 96. **a' my:** i.e., of my

100. **argosy:** large trading ship

112. **divers:** several

112–13. **in my company to Venice:** i.e., in the group with whom I traveled to Venice

113–14. **cannot . . . break:** i.e., will surely go bankrupt

119. **Out upon her!:** i.e., curses on her!

125. **fee me:** i.e., hire me (to arrest Antonio, if the bond is forfeited); **Bespeak:** arrange for

ducats in her coffin. No news of them? Why so? And 90
I know not what's spent in the search! Why, thou
loss upon loss! The thief gone with so much, and so
much to find the thief, and no satisfaction, no
revenge, nor no ill luck stirring but what lights a' my
shoulders, no sighs but a' my breathing, no tears but 95
a' my shedding.

TUBAL   Yes, other men have ill luck, too. Antonio, as I
heard in Genoa—

SHYLOCK   What, what, what? Ill luck, ill luck?

TUBAL   —hath an argosy cast away coming from Tri- 100
polis.

SHYLOCK   I thank God, I thank God! Is it true, is it true?

TUBAL   I spoke with some of the sailors that escaped
the wrack.

SHYLOCK   I thank thee, good Tubal. Good news, good 105
news! Ha, ha, ⌜heard⌝ in Genoa—

TUBAL   Your daughter spent in Genoa, as I heard, one
night fourscore ducats.

SHYLOCK   Thou stick'st a dagger in me. I shall never
see my gold again. Fourscore ducats at a sitting, 110
fourscore ducats!

TUBAL   There came divers of Antonio's creditors in my
company to Venice that swear he cannot choose
but break.

SHYLOCK   I am very glad of it. I'll plague him, I'll 115
torture him. I am glad of it.

TUBAL   One of them showed me a ring that he had of
your daughter for a monkey.

SHYLOCK   Out upon her! Thou torturest me, Tubal. It
was my ⌜turquoise!⌝ I had it of Leah when I was a 120
bachelor. I would not have given it for a wilderness
of monkeys.

TUBAL   But Antonio is certainly undone.

SHYLOCK   Nay, that's true, that's very true. Go, Tubal,
fee me an officer. Bespeak him a fortnight before. I 125

126. **him:** i.e., Antonio

127. **make what merchandise I will:** i.e., drive any bargain I wish (for lending money)

3.2 Portia advises Bassanio to postpone choosing for fear he should make the wrong choice. Bassanio declares himself unable to live in uncertainty. Portia is overjoyed when Bassanio correctly chooses the lead chest containing her picture. Giving Bassanio a ring as a symbolic act to indicate her giving to him both herself and everything that is hers, Portia insists that he treasure the ring. Gratiano announces that he and Nerissa will also marry. Salerio, Lorenzo, and Jessica arrive with the news of Antonio's financial ruin and the apparently certain destruction that he will soon suffer at Shylock's hands. Portia offers to pay the debt many times over and tells Bassanio to return to Venice immediately after their wedding to save Antonio.

———————

2. **hazard:** i.e., venture to choose among the chests; **in choosing wrong:** i.e., if you choose wrong

5. **would not:** i.e., do not wish to

6. **quality:** way, manner

8. **yet a maiden . . . thought:** perhaps, a maiden cannot (or should not) put her thoughts into words; or, perhaps Portia is saying that her words perfectly reflect her thoughts

11. **am forsworn:** i.e., perjure myself

12. **So . . . So:** that . . . thus

(continued)

will have the heart of him if he forfeit, for were he
out of Venice I can make what merchandise I will.
Go, Tubal, and meet me at our synagogue. Go, good
Tubal, at our synagogue, Tubal.

They exit.

⌈Scene 2⌉
Enter Bassanio, Portia, and all their trains, Gratiano,
⌈*Nerissa.*⌉

PORTIA
I pray you tarry, pause a day or two
Before you hazard, for in choosing wrong
I lose your company; therefore forbear a while.
There's something tells me (but it is not love)
I would not lose you, and you know yourself   5
Hate counsels not in such a quality.
But lest you should not understand me well
(And yet a maiden hath no tongue but thought)
I would detain you here some month or two
Before you venture for me. I could teach you   10
How to choose right, but then I am forsworn.
So will I never be. So may you miss me.
But if you do, you'll make me wish a sin,
That I had been forsworn. Beshrew your eyes,
They have o'erlooked me and divided me.   15
One half of me is yours, the other half yours—
Mine own, I would say—but if mine, then yours,
And so all yours. O, these naughty times
Puts bars between the owners and their rights!
And so though yours, not yours. Prove it so,   20
Let Fortune go to hell for it, not I.
I speak too long, but 'tis to peize the time,
To eche it, and to draw it out in length,
To stay you from election.

14. **That:** namely, that; **Beshrew:** literally, curse, but the sense here is less strong

15. **o'erlooked:** (1) bewitched; (2) perused

18. **naughty:** evil

19. **Puts:** i.e., put; **bars:** i.e., impediments

20–21. **Prove it so . . . hell for it:** i.e., if I do not chance to be yours, let Fortune be blamed

22. **peize:** load, burden, weigh down

23. **eche:** increase, add to

24. **stay . . . election:** delay your choosing

26. **upon the rack:** i.e., as if being tortured (The rack was an instrument of torture used to extract confessions from alleged criminals, such as those who had been accused of treason.)

30. **fear:** i.e., fear for, doubt

32. **as:** i.e., as between

34. **enforcèd:** under compulsion

36. **confess and live:** inverting the proverb "Confess and be hanged"

41. **let me to:** i.e., allow me to approach

46. **a swanlike end:** Swans were thought to sing as they died.

48. **more proper:** i.e., as more appropriate

51. **flourish:** trumpet blast

53. **in:** i.e., at

55. **he:** i.e., Bassanio

BASSANIO   Let me choose,   25
  For as I am, I live upon the rack.
PORTIA
  Upon the rack, Bassanio? Then confess
  What treason there is mingled with your love.
BASSANIO
  None but that ugly treason of mistrust,
  Which makes me fear th' enjoying of my love.   30
  There may as well be amity and life
  'Tween snow and fire, as treason and my love.
PORTIA
  Ay, but I fear you speak upon the rack
  Where men enforcèd do speak anything.
BASSANIO
  Promise me life and I'll confess the truth.   35
PORTIA
  Well, then, confess and live.
BASSANIO   "Confess and love"
  Had been the very sum of my confession.
  O happy torment, when my torturer
  Doth teach me answers for deliverance!   40
  But let me to my fortune and the caskets.
PORTIA
  Away, then. I am locked in one of them.
  If you do love me, you will find me out.—
  Nerissa and the rest, stand all aloof.
  Let music sound while he doth make his choice.   45
  Then if he lose he makes a swanlike end,
  Fading in music. That the comparison
  May stand more proper, my eye shall be the stream
  And wat'ry deathbed for him. He may win,
  And what is music then? Then music is   50
  Even as the flourish when true subjects bow
  To a new-crownèd monarch. Such it is
  As are those dulcet sounds in break of day
  That creep into the dreaming bridegroom's ear
  And summon him to marriage. Now he goes,   55

56. **presence:** bearing, dignity

57. **Alcides:** Hercules, the mythological hero who rescued Hesione, the daughter of the king of Troy, from a sea monster, to whom she was about to be sacrificed by her father to appease the god Neptune

58. **virgin tribute:** i.e., sacrifice of a virgin

59. **I stand for sacrifice:** Portia imagines herself in the role of Hesione.

60. **aloof:** apart; **Dardanian:** Trojan

61. **blearèd:** tear-streaked

62. **issue:** result

63. **Live thou:** i.e., if you live

64. **thou that mak'st the fray:** i.e., you who fight

65. **fancy:** i.e., desire

72. **knell:** the solemn bell marking a death

76. **still:** always; **ornament:** outward show or display (See also at lines 82 and 99.)

78. **gracious:** i.e., graceful

80. **sober brow:** i.e., someone with a solemn expression and appearance

81. **approve . . . a text:** demonstrate its truth by quoting from the Bible

83. **simple:** purely itself, unmixed

84. **his:** its

86. **yet:** nevertheless

87. **Hercules:** a hero of extraordinary strength; **Mars:** god of war

With no less presence but with much more love
Than young Alcides when he did redeem
The virgin tribute paid by howling Troy
To the sea-monster. I stand for sacrifice;
The rest aloof are the Dardanian wives,   60
With blearèd visages, come forth to view
The issue of th' exploit. Go, Hercules!
Live thou, I live. With much much more dismay
I view the fight than thou that mak'st the fray.

A song the whilst Bassanio comments on
the caskets to himself.

    Tell me where is fancy bred,   65
    Or in the heart, or in the head?
    How begot, how nourishèd?
      Reply, reply.
    It is engendered in the eye,
    With gazing fed, and fancy dies   70
    In the cradle where it lies.
    Let us all ring fancy's knell.
    I'll begin it.—Ding, dong, bell.

ALL   *Ding, dong, bell.*
BASSANIO
So may the outward shows be least themselves;   75
The world is still deceived with ornament.
In law, what plea so tainted and corrupt
But, being seasoned with a gracious voice,
Obscures the show of evil? In religion,
What damnèd error but some sober brow   80
Will bless it and approve it with a text,
Hiding the grossness with fair ornament?
There is no ⌜vice⌝ so simple but assumes
Some mark of virtue on his outward parts.
How many cowards whose hearts are all as false   85
As ⌜stairs⌝ of sand, wear yet upon their chins
The beards of Hercules and frowning Mars,

88. inward searched: i.e., if their bodies were examined within; **livers white as milk:** A white liver was said to be the mark of a coward.

89. excrement: outgrowth (i.e., the beard)

90. redoubted: feared, dreaded

93. lightest: least respectable (a pun)

94. crispèd: curled; **locks:** strands of hair

96. supposèd fairness: what is thought to be beauty; or, counterfeit beauty

97–98. dowry . . . sepulcher: i.e., a wig made of hair from a head that is now in the grave **dowry:** endowment

99. guilèd: treacherous

101. an Indian beauty: one with a dark complexion, who therefore would not match the stereotype of fair-skinned beauty then in force

105. Midas: the mythological king whose greed for gold destroyed him when everything he touched, including his food, turned to gold

106–7. pale . . . man: silver, which functioned as currency **common drudge:** servant to everyone

107. meager: poor

109. moves: i.e., affects me emotionally

112. As: i.e., such as; **rash:** i.e., rashly, heedlessly

115. rain: i.e., rain down (The word would also be heard as *rein*, control.); **scant:** withhold or reduce

119. counterfeit: image, picture

119–20. What demigod . . . creation?: i.e., what artist has so nearly duplicated Portia as to seem a god?

Who inward searched have livers white as milk,
And these assume but valor's excrement
To render them redoubted. Look on beauty, 90
And you shall see 'tis purchased by the weight,
Which therein works a miracle in nature,
Making them lightest that wear most of it.
So are those crispèd snaky golden locks,
Which maketh such wanton gambols with the wind 95
Upon supposèd fairness, often known
To be the dowry of a second head,
The skull that bred them in the sepulcher.
Thus ornament is but the guilèd shore
To a most dangerous sea, the beauteous scarf 100
Veiling an Indian beauty; in a word,
The seeming truth which cunning times put on
To entrap the wisest. Therefore, then, thou gaudy
    gold,
Hard food for Midas, I will none of thee. 105
Nor none of thee, thou pale and common drudge
'Tween man and man. But thou, thou meager lead,
Which rather threaten'st than dost promise aught,
Thy paleness moves me more than eloquence,
And here choose I. Joy be the consequence! 110
⌐*Bassanio is given a key.*⌐

PORTIA, ⌐*aside*⌐
How all the other passions fleet to air,
As doubtful thoughts and rash embraced despair,
And shudd'ring fear, and green-eyed jealousy!
O love, be moderate, allay thy ecstasy,
In measure rain thy joy, scant this excess! 115
I feel too much thy blessing. Make it less,
For fear I surfeit.
                    ⌐*Bassanio opens the lead casket.*⌐
BASSANIO   What find I here?
Fair Portia's counterfeit! What demigod
Hath come so near creation? Move these eyes? 120

121. **Or whether:** i.e., or
123. **bar:** i.e., barrier (here, Portia's breath)
124. **such sweet friends:** i.e., Portia's lips
127. **Faster:** more securely
130. **unfurnished:** i.e., unmatched with the second eye, because the artist could no longer see to paint it
131. **shadow:** picture
133. **substance:** i.e., Portia herself
134. **continent:** i.e., container
136. **Chance as fair:** enjoy as good luck
137. **this fortune:** i.e., Portia
140. **hold . . . for:** regard . . . as
144. **by note:** i.e., authorized by the scroll
145. **prize:** match, athletic contest

Or whether, riding on the balls of mine,
Seem they in motion? Here are severed lips
Parted with sugar breath; so sweet a bar
Should sunder such sweet friends. Here in her hairs
The painter plays the spider, and hath woven   125
A golden mesh t' entrap the hearts of men
Faster than gnats in cobwebs. But her eyes!
How could he see to do them? Having made one,
Methinks it should have power to steal both his
And leave itself unfurnished. Yet look how far   130
The substance of my praise doth wrong this shadow
In underprizing it, so far this shadow
Doth limp behind the substance. Here's the scroll,
The continent and summary of my fortune.
⌜*He reads the scroll.*⌝
              You that choose not by the view   135
              Chance as fair and choose as true.
              Since this fortune falls to you,
              Be content and seek no new.
              If you be well pleased with this
              And hold your fortune for your bliss,   140
              Turn you where your lady is,
              And claim her with a loving kiss.
A gentle scroll! Fair lady, by your leave,
I come by note to give and to receive.
Like one of two contending in a prize   145
That thinks he hath done well in people's eyes,
Hearing applause and universal shout,
Giddy in spirit, still gazing in a doubt
Whether those peals of praise be his or no,
So, thrice-fair lady, stand I even so,   150
As doubtful whether what I see be true,
Until confirmed, signed, ratified by you.
PORTIA
You see me, Lord Bassanio, where I stand,
Such as I am. Though for myself alone

160. **livings:** estates, possessions

161. **account:** computation (This begins a set of commercial terms: **sum, gross.**)

162. **to term in gross:** to identify in general terms

171. **But now:** i.e., just a moment ago

178. **be my . . . on you:** provide me with a position of superiority from which to cry out against you

185. **blent:** blended

186. **wild:** wilderness; **save of:** except

I would not be ambitious in my wish   155
To wish myself much better, yet for you
I would be trebled twenty times myself,
A thousand times more fair, ten thousand times
More rich, that only to stand high in your account
I might in virtues, beauties, livings, friends,   160
Exceed account. But the full sum of me
Is sum of something, which, to term in gross,
Is an unlessoned girl, unschooled, unpracticed;
Happy in this, she is not yet so old
But she may learn; happier than this,   165
She is not bred so dull but she can learn;
Happiest of all, is that her gentle spirit
Commits itself to yours to be directed
As from her lord, her governor, her king.
Myself, and what is mine, to you and yours   170
Is now converted. But now I was the lord
Of this fair mansion, master of my servants,
Queen o'er myself; and even now, but now,
This house, these servants, and this same myself
Are yours, my lord's. I give them with this ring,   175
                    ⌜*Handing him a ring.*⌝
Which, when you part from, lose, or give away,
Let it presage the ruin of your love,
And be my vantage to exclaim on you.

BASSANIO
Madam, you have bereft me of all words.
Only my blood speaks to you in my veins,   180
And there is such confusion in my powers
As after some oration fairly spoke
By a belovèd prince there doth appear
Among the buzzing pleasèd multitude,
Where every something being blent together   185
Turns to a wild of nothing, save of joy
Expressed and not expressed. But when this ring
Parts from this finger, then parts life from hence.
O, then be bold to say Bassanio's dead!

191. **That:** i.e., we who

195. **none from me:** perhaps, no more from me than I have already wished you; or, perhaps, none away from me (i.e., your happiness will not take away from mine)

197. **bargain:** contract; **faith:** i.e., vow

199. **so:** if

202. **maid:** i.e., Nerissa, who is Portia's lady-in-waiting or "waiting gentlewoman," an attendant who is also a confidante

203. **intermission:** delay, waiting around

206. **as the matter falls:** i.e., as it happens

207. **sweat:** i.e., did sweat

208. **my . . . roof:** i.e., the roof of my mouth

211–12. **your fortune / Achieved:** i.e., it was your good fortune to win

214. **so:** if; **withal:** i.e., with it

216. **faith:** i.e., in faith (an oath)

218. **play . . . boy:** i.e., wager with them about which couple will first have a boy

NERISSA
  My lord and lady, it is now our time,   190
  That have stood by and seen our wishes prosper,
  To cry "Good joy, good joy, my lord and lady!"
GRATIANO
  My Lord Bassanio, and my gentle lady,
  I wish you all the joy that you can wish,
  For I am sure you can wish none from me.   195
  And when your honors mean to solemnize
  The bargain of your faith, I do beseech you
  Even at that time I may be married too.
BASSANIO
  With all my heart, so thou canst get a wife.
GRATIANO
  I thank your Lordship, you have got me one.   200
  My eyes, my lord, can look as swift as yours:
  You saw the mistress, I beheld the maid.
  You loved, I loved; for intermission
  No more pertains to me, my lord, than you.
  Your fortune stood upon the caskets there,   205
  And so did mine, too, as the matter falls.
  For wooing here until I sweat again,
  And swearing till my very roof was dry
  With oaths of love, at last (if promise last)
  I got a promise of this fair one here   210
  To have her love, provided that your fortune
  Achieved her mistress.
PORTIA   Is this true, Nerissa?
NERISSA
  Madam, it is, so you stand pleased withal.
BASSANIO
  And do you, Gratiano, mean good faith?   215
GRATIANO   Yes, faith, my lord.
BASSANIO
  Our feast shall be much honored in your marriage.
GRATIANO   We'll play with them the first boy for a
    thousand ducats.

220. **stake down:** i.e., put our money on the table

221-22. **and stake down:** i.e., if my "stake" is down (a bawdy joke)

226-27. **If . . . welcome:** i.e., if the brief time I have been in my new position here gives me the power to welcome you

229. **very:** i.e., true

233. **My . . . seen:** i.e., I did not set out to see

235. **past:** beyond

245. **estate:** condition

246. **cheer yond stranger:** i.e., greet Jessica

NERISSA　What, and stake down?　　　　　　　　　　220
GRATIANO　No, we shall ne'er win at that sport and
　stake down.

*Enter Lorenzo, Jessica, and Salerio, a messenger from
　　　　　　　　　Venice.*

　But who comes here? Lorenzo and his infidel?
　What, and my old Venetian friend Salerio?
BASSANIO
　Lorenzo and Salerio, welcome hither—　　　　　225
　If that the youth of my new int'rest here
　Have power to bid you welcome. ⌐To Portia.⌐ By
　　your leave,
　I bid my very friends and countrymen,
　Sweet Portia, welcome.　　　　　　　　　　230
PORTIA
　So do I, my lord. They are entirely welcome.
LORENZO, ⌐to Bassanio⌐
　I thank your Honor. For my part, my lord,
　My purpose was not to have seen you here,
　But meeting with Salerio by the way,
　He did entreat me past all saying nay　　　　235
　To come with him along.
SALERIO　　　　　　　　　I did, my lord,
　And I have reason for it. ⌐Handing him a paper.⌐
　　　　　　　　　　Signior Antonio
　Commends him to you.　　　　　　　　　240
BASSANIO　　　　　　　　Ere I ope his letter,
　I pray you tell me how my good friend doth.
SALERIO
　Not sick, my lord, unless it be in mind,
　Nor well, unless in mind. His letter there
　Will show you his estate.　　　　　　　　245
　　　　　　　⌐Bassanio⌐ opens the letter.
GRATIANO
　Nerissa, cheer yond stranger, bid her welcome.—
　Your hand, Salerio. What's the news from Venice?

250. **Jasons . . . Fleece:** See note to 1.1.178.

251. **would:** wish; **fleece:** perhaps a quibble on "fleets"

252. **shrewd:** serious, harsh

255. **dead . . . nothing:** i.e., is dead, for nothing else

256. **turn:** i.e., change

257. **constant:** steadfast

268. **Rating:** evaluating

270. **state:** fortune, estate, property

272, 273. **engaged:** pledged

273. **mere:** utter, absolute

275. **as:** i.e., as if it were

278. **not one hit:** i.e., did not one succeed

How doth that royal merchant, good Antonio?
I know he will be glad of our success.
We are the Jasons, we have won the Fleece.   250

SALERIO
I would you had won the fleece that he hath lost.

PORTIA
There are some shrewd contents in yond same
    paper
That steals the color from Bassanio's cheek.
Some dear friend dead, else nothing in the world   255
Could turn so much the constitution
Of any constant man. What, worse and worse?—
With leave, Bassanio, I am half yourself,
And I must freely have the half of anything
That this same paper brings you.   260

BASSANIO   O sweet Portia,
Here are a few of the unpleasant'st words
That ever blotted paper. Gentle lady,
When I did first impart my love to you,
I freely told you all the wealth I had   265
Ran in my veins: I was a gentleman.
And then I told you true; and yet, dear lady,
Rating myself at nothing, you shall see
How much I was a braggart. When I told you
My state was nothing, I should then have told you   270
That I was worse than nothing; for indeed
I have engaged myself to a dear friend,
Engaged my friend to his mere enemy
To feed my means. Here is a letter, lady,
The paper as the body of my friend,   275
And every word in it a gaping wound
Issuing life blood.—But is it true, Salerio?
Hath all his ventures failed? What, not one hit?
From Tripolis, from Mexico and England,
From Lisbon, Barbary, and India,   280
And not one vessel 'scape the dreadful touch
Of merchant-marring rocks?

284. **should:** i.e., would
285. **present money:** i.e., money available
286. **He:** i.e., Shylock
288. **keen:** fierce, cruel; **confound:** destroy
289. **plies:** applies pressure to
290. **impeach . . . state:** i.e., accuse the state of tyranny
292–93. **magnificoes . . . port:** i.e., the most dignified of Venetian nobles
293. **persuaded:** argued
294. **envious:** malicious
294–95. **plea / Of:** demand for
300. **he:** i.e., Antonio
305. **best conditioned:** best tempered
306. **courtesies:** kindnesses
312. **deface:** cancel

Magnificoes. (3.2.292)
From Giacomo Franco, *Habiti d'huomeni* . . . (1609?).

SALERIO   Not one, my lord.
  Besides, it should appear that if he had
  The present money to discharge the Jew,   285
  He would not take it. Never did I know
  A creature that did bear the shape of man
  So keen and greedy to confound a man.
  He plies the Duke at morning and at night,
  And doth impeach the freedom of the state   290
  If they deny him justice. Twenty merchants,
  The Duke himself, and the magnificoes
  Of greatest port have all persuaded with him,
  But none can drive him from the envious plea
  Of forfeiture, of justice, and his bond.   295

JESSICA
  When I was with him, I have heard him swear
  To Tubal and to Chus, his countrymen,
  That he would rather have Antonio's flesh
  Than twenty times the value of the sum
  That he did owe him. And I know, my lord,   300
  If law, authority, and power deny not,
  It will go hard with poor Antonio.

PORTIA
  Is it your dear friend that is thus in trouble?

BASSANIO
  The dearest friend to me, the kindest man,
  The best conditioned and unwearied spirit   305
  In doing courtesies, and one in whom
  The ancient Roman honor more appears
  Than any that draws breath in Italy.

PORTIA   What sum owes he the Jew?

BASSANIO
  For me, three thousand ducats.   310

PORTIA   What, no more?
  Pay him six thousand and deface the bond.
  Double six thousand and then treble that,
  Before a friend of this description
  Shall lose a hair through Bassanio's fault.   315

324. **shall hence:** i.e., shall depart

325. **cheer:** expression

326. **dear . . . dear:** expensively . . . dearly

328. **miscarried:** i.e., been wrecked

329. **estate:** fortune

332. **but:** only

332–33. **Notwithstanding . . . pleasure:** i.e., in any case, do as you please

336. **good leave:** consent

339. **be . . . twain:** be placed between the two of us

3.3 Antonio seeks out Shylock in an effort to get the moneylender to listen to him. But Shylock insists that the terms of the bond be fulfilled. Antonio is resigned to death provided Bassanio is there to see him die.

First go with me to church and call me wife,
And then away to Venice to your friend!
For never shall you lie by Portia's side
With an unquiet soul. You shall have gold
To pay the petty debt twenty times over.   320
When it is paid, bring your true friend along.
My maid Nerissa and myself meantime
Will live as maids and widows. Come, away,
For you shall hence upon your wedding day.
Bid your friends welcome, show a merry cheer;   325
Since you are dear bought, I will love you dear.
But let me hear the letter of your friend.

⌜BASSANIO *reads*⌝

> *Sweet Bassanio, my ships have all miscarried, my*
> *creditors grow cruel, my estate is very low, my bond to*
> *the Jew is forfeit, and since in paying it, it is impossible* 330
> *I should live, all debts are cleared between you and I if*
> *I might but see you at my death. Notwithstanding, use*
> *your pleasure. If your love do not persuade you to*
> *come, let not my letter.*

PORTIA
O love, dispatch all business and begone!   335

BASSANIO
Since I have your good leave to go away,
I will make haste. But till I come again,
No bed shall e'er be guilty of my stay,
Nor rest be interposer 'twixt us twain.

                                                               They exit.

⌜Scene 3⌝
Enter ⌜Shylock,⌝ the Jew, and ⌜Solanio,⌝ and Antonio,
and the Jailer.

SHYLOCK
Jailer, look to him. Tell not me of mercy.

2. **gratis:** without requiring interest
10. **naughty:** wicked; **fond:** foolish
11. **abroad:** out in public
19. **impenetrable:** impervious to argument
20. **kept:** lived
22. **bootless:** useless
28. **grant:** allow; **to hold:** i.e., to be put into effect
29–34. The loose construction of this sentence creates some difficulty. It seems to say that the Duke cannot interfere with the law without thereby denying all foreigners, including Jews, the privilege under the law that encourages all nations to trade in Venice and that thus makes Venice the prosperous city it is.
30. **commodity:** benefits, privileges
31. **it:** i.e., the course of the law
32. **impeach:** discredit
33. **Since that:** i.e., since

This is the fool that lent out money gratis.
Jailer, look to him.

ANTONIO   Hear me yet, good Shylock—

SHYLOCK
I'll have my bond. Speak not against my bond.   5
I have sworn an oath that I will have my bond.
Thou call'dst me dog before thou hadst a cause,
But since I am a dog, beware my fangs.
The Duke shall grant me justice.—I do wonder,
Thou naughty jailer, that thou art so fond   10
To come abroad with him at his request.

ANTONIO   I pray thee, hear me speak—

SHYLOCK
I'll have my bond. I will not hear thee speak.
I'll have my bond, and therefore speak no more.
I'll not be made a soft and dull-eyed fool,   15
To shake the head, relent, and sigh, and yield
To Christian intercessors. Follow not!
I'll have no speaking. I will have my bond. ⌜*He*⌝ *exits.*

SOLANIO
It is the most impenetrable cur
That ever kept with men.   20

ANTONIO   Let him alone.
I'll follow him no more with bootless prayers.
He seeks my life. His reason well I know:
I oft delivered from his forfeitures
Many that have at times made moan to me.   25
Therefore he hates me.

SOLANIO   I am sure the Duke
Will never grant this forfeiture to hold.

ANTONIO
The Duke cannot deny the course of law,
For the commodity that strangers have   30
With us in Venice, if it be denied,
Will much impeach the justice of the state,
Since that the trade and profit of the city

35. **bated:** abated, shrunk

3.4 Portia entrusts the management of her household to Lorenzo and pretends to leave with Nerissa for a monastery. She sends a messenger to Dr. Bellario of Padua and tells Nerissa that they, in disguise as men, will follow their husbands to Venice.

————————

2. **conceit:** understanding, conception
3. **amity:** friendship; **which:** i.e., your understanding
7. **lover:** This word in the Renaissance could have the meaning of friend or well-wisher, as well as its more customary meaning.
9. **Than . . . you:** i.e., than the kindness you habitually display can make you
12. **waste:** pass
14. **must be needs:** i.e., must be
15. **lineaments:** characteristics
17. **bosom:** confidential
20. **semblance of my soul:** i.e., Antonio, who is the image of Bassanio, Portia's "soul"

Consisteth of all nations. Therefore go.
These griefs and losses have so bated me   35
That I shall hardly spare a pound of flesh
Tomorrow to my bloody creditor.—
Well, jailer, on.—Pray God Bassanio come
To see me pay his debt, and then I care not.

They exit.

⌜Scene 4⌝
Enter Portia, Nerissa, Lorenzo, Jessica, and ⌜*Balthazar,*⌝
a man of Portia's.

LORENZO
Madam, although I speak it in your presence,
You have a noble and a true conceit
Of godlike amity, which appears most strongly
In bearing thus the absence of your lord.
But if you knew to whom you show this honor,   5
How true a gentleman you send relief,
How dear a lover of my lord your husband,
I know you would be prouder of the work
Than customary bounty can enforce you.
PORTIA
I never did repent for doing good,   10
Nor shall not now; for in companions
That do converse and waste the time together,
Whose souls do bear an equal yoke of love,
There must be needs a like proportion
Of lineaments, of manners, and of spirit;   15
Which makes me think that this Antonio,
Being the bosom lover of my lord,
Must needs be like my lord. If it be so,
How little is the cost I have bestowed
In purchasing the semblance of my soul   20
From out the state of hellish cruelty!

25. **husbandry and manage:** i.e., management

33. **deny this imposition:** refuse to accept the trust that I wish to impose on you

36. **with . . . heart:** a polite phrase indicating assent

47. **honest true:** honest and faithful

49. **endeavor:** strenuous effort

"Sultan Solyman." (2.1.27)
From Paolo Giovio, *Nouocomensis Episcopi* . . . (1575).

This comes too near the praising of myself;
Therefore no more of it. Hear other things:
Lorenzo, I commit into your hands
The husbandry and manage of my house   25
Until my lord's return. For mine own part,
I have toward heaven breathed a secret vow
To live in prayer and contemplation,
Only attended by Nerissa here,
Until her husband and my lord's return.   30
There is a monastery two miles off,
And there we will abide. I do desire you
Not to deny this imposition,
The which my love and some necessity
Now lays upon you.   35

LORENZO   Madam, with all my heart.
I shall obey you in all fair commands.

PORTIA
My people do already know my mind
And will acknowledge you and Jessica
In place of Lord Bassanio and myself.   40
So fare you well till we shall meet again.

LORENZO
Fair thoughts and happy hours attend on you!

JESSICA
I wish your Ladyship all heart's content.

PORTIA
I thank you for your wish, and am well pleased
To wish it back on you. Fare you well, Jessica.   45
⌜*Lorenzo and Jessica*⌝ *exit.*
Now, Balthazar,
As I have ever found thee honest true,
So let me find thee still: take this same letter,
And use thou all th' endeavor of a man
In speed to ⌜Padua.⌝ See thou render this   50
Into my ⌜cousin's⌝ hands, Doctor Bellario.
⌜*She gives him a paper.*⌝

52. **look what:** whatever

54. **imagined:** i.e., all imaginable

55. **traject:** i.e., *traghetto*, Italian for "ferry"

58. **convenient:** due, appropriate

63. **habit:** dress, costume

64. **accomplishèd:** equipped

65. **that we lack:** that which we lack (i.e., male organs); **hold thee any wager:** bet you anything

68. **braver:** finer

69–70. **speak . . . voice:** i.e., speak in a piping voice as if I were an adolescent boy

70. **mincing:** small and dainty

72. **quaint:** clever

75. **I . . . withal:** i.e., I could do nothing about it

78–79. **I . . . twelvemonth:** i.e., I finished being a schoolboy more than a year ago

80. **raw:** crude, immature; **jacks:** fellows

82. **turn to men:** Nerissa means "turn ourselves into men." Portia responds as if the phrase meant "turn to men for sexual satisfaction." (See 1.3.89 for this "lewd" use of the phrase.)

And look what notes and garments he doth give
  thee,
Bring them, I pray thee, with imagined speed
Unto the ⌈traject,⌉ to the common ferry   55
Which trades to Venice. Waste no time in words,
But get thee gone. I shall be there before thee.

BALTHAZAR
Madam, I go with all convenient speed.   ⌈*He exits.*⌉

PORTIA
Come on, Nerissa, I have work in hand
That you yet know not of. We'll see our husbands 60
Before they think of us.

NERISSA   Shall they see us?

PORTIA
They shall, Nerissa, but in such a habit
That they shall think we are accomplishèd
With that we lack. I'll hold thee any wager, 65
When we are both accoutered like young men,
I'll prove the prettier fellow of the two,
And wear my dagger with the braver grace,
And speak between the change of man and boy
With a reed voice, and turn two mincing steps 70
Into a manly stride, and speak of frays
Like a fine bragging youth, and tell quaint lies
How honorable ladies sought my love,
Which I denying, they fell sick and died—
I could not do withal!—then I'll repent, 75
And wish, for all that, that I had not killed them.
And twenty of these puny lies I'll tell,
That men shall swear I have discontinued school
Above a twelvemonth. I have within my mind
A thousand raw tricks of these bragging jacks 80
Which I will practice.

NERISSA   Why, shall we turn to men?

PORTIA   Fie, what a question's that,
If thou wert near a lewd interpreter!

85. **device:** plan
86. **stays:** waits

3.5 Lancelet, the clown, makes jokes at the expense of Jessica and then Lorenzo. Jessica praises Portia and jokes with Lorenzo.

————————

3. **fear you:** i.e., fear for you
4. **agitation:** i.e., perhaps, cogitation
7. **bastard:** counterfeit, not genuine (Jessica picks up the usual meaning of the word at line 12.)
11. **got:** begot
15–16. **Scylla . . . Charybdis:** Mariners navigating the Straits of Messina had to avoid simultaneously the rock of Scylla and the whirlpool Charybdis. "To be caught between Scylla and Charybdis" is an expression meaning that one is in a hopeless dilemma.
17. **gone:** destroyed
21. **enow:** enough
22. **one by another:** i.e., together
23. **hogs, pork:** food forbidden by Jewish dietary law
24. **rasher:** i.e., of bacon

But come, I'll tell thee all my whole device   85
When I am in my coach, which stays for us
At the park gate; and therefore haste away,
For we must measure twenty miles today.

They exit.

⌜Scene 5⌝
Enter ⌜Lancelet, the⌝ Clown and Jessica.

LANCELET   Yes, truly, for look you, the sins of the father
are to be laid upon the children. Therefore I
promise you I fear you. I was always plain with you,
and so now I speak my agitation of the matter.
Therefore be o' good cheer, for truly I think you   5
are damned. There is but one hope in it that can do
you any good, and that is but a kind of bastard hope
neither.

JESSICA   And what hope is that, I pray thee?

LANCELET   Marry, you may partly hope that your father   10
got you not, that you are not the Jew's daughter.

JESSICA   That were a kind of bastard hope indeed; so
the sins of my mother should be visited upon me!

LANCELET   Truly, then, I fear you are damned both by
father and mother; thus when I shun Scylla your   15
father, I fall into Charybdis your mother. Well, you
are gone both ways.

JESSICA   I shall be saved by my husband. He hath made
me a Christian.

LANCELET   Truly the more to blame he! We were Chris-   20
tians enow before, e'en as many as could well live
one by another. This making of Christians will
raise the price of hogs. If we grow all to be pork
eaters, we shall not shortly have a rasher on the
coals for money.   25

Enter Lorenzo.

30. **fear:** suspect

31. **out:** at odds

38. **Moor:** pronounced "more," and so Lancelet's wordplay **more than reason** (lines 39–40), i.e., more than she reasonably should be

40. **honest:** chaste

42. **play . . . word:** i.e., make puns, engage in wordplay

43–44. **best . . . silence:** surest sign of intelligence will soon be silence

47. **stomachs:** appetites

50, 52. **cover:** i.e., set the table

53. **I know my duty:** Lancelet now takes **cover** to mean "Put on your hat." It was his duty to remain uncovered in the presence of his superiors.

54. **quarreling with occasion:** disputing at every opportunity

60. **table:** supply of food, fare

61. **meat:** food; **covered:** served in covered dishes

JESSICA   I'll tell my husband, Lancelet, what you say.
Here he ⌜comes.⌝

LORENZO   I shall grow jealous of you shortly, Lancelet,
if you thus get my wife into corners!

JESSICA   Nay, you need not fear us, Lorenzo. Lancelet   30
and I are out. He tells me flatly there's no mercy for
me in heaven because I am a Jew's daughter; and
he says you are no good member of the common-
wealth, for in converting Jews to Christians you
raise the price of pork.   35

LORENZO   I shall answer that better to the common-
wealth than you can the getting up of the Negro's
belly! The Moor is with child by you, Lancelet.

LANCELET   It is much that the Moor should be more
than reason; but if she be less than an honest   40
woman, she is indeed more than I took her for.

LORENZO   How every fool can play upon the word! I
think the best grace of wit will shortly turn into
silence, and discourse grow commendable in none
only but parrots. Go in, sirrah, bid them prepare for   45
dinner.

LANCELET   That is done, sir. They have all stomachs.

LORENZO   Goodly Lord, what a wit-snapper are you!
Then bid them prepare dinner.

LANCELET   That is done too, sir, only "cover" is the   50
word.

LORENZO   Will you cover, then, sir?

LANCELET   Not so, sir, neither! I know my duty.

LORENZO   Yet more quarreling with occasion! Wilt
thou show the whole wealth of thy wit in an   55
instant? I pray thee understand a plain man in his
plain meaning: go to thy fellows, bid them cover the
table, serve in the meat, and we will come in to
dinner.

LANCELET   For the table, sir, it shall be served in; for   60
the meat, sir, it shall be covered; for your coming in

62. **humors and conceits:** whims and fancies

64. **suited:** fitted, adapted

67. **A many fools:** many a fool; **stand in better place:** enjoy higher social status

68. **Garnished like him:** i.e., perhaps, equipped with vocabularies like his

68–69. **for a tricksy word / Defy the matter:** for the sake of wordplay, digress from the topic

69. **How cheer'st thou:** i.e., how are you

72. **meet:** fitting

76. **merit it:** i.e., deserve or earn such joy

79. **lay:** should stake

80. **else:** more

81. **Pawned with:** bet along with

86. **anon:** soon

87. **stomach:** appetite (for food); desire (to praise)

91. **set you forth:** i.e., (1) serve you up as if you were a dish; (2) praise you in detail

to dinner, sir, why, let it be as humors and conceits
shall govern.   ⌜*Lancelet*⌝ *exits.*
LORENZO
O dear discretion, how his words are suited!
The fool hath planted in his memory   65
An army of good words, and I do know
A many fools that stand in better place,
Garnished like him, that for a tricksy word
Defy the matter. How cheer'st thou, Jessica?
And now, good sweet, say thy opinion   70
How dost thou like the Lord Bassanio's wife?
JESSICA
Past all expressing. It is very meet
The Lord Bassanio live an upright life,
For having such a blessing in his lady
He finds the joys of heaven here on earth,   75
And if on earth he do not ⌜merit⌝ it,
In reason he should never come to heaven.
Why, if two gods should play some heavenly match,
And on the wager lay two earthly women,
And Portia one, there must be something else   80
Pawned with the other, for the poor rude world
Hath not her fellow.
LORENZO   Even such a husband
Hast thou of me as she is for ⌜a⌝ wife.
JESSICA
Nay, but ask my opinion too of that!   85
LORENZO
I will anon. First let us go to dinner.
JESSICA
Nay, let me praise you while I have a stomach!
LORENZO
No, pray thee, let it serve for table talk.
Then howsome'er thou speak'st, 'mong other things
I shall digest it.   90
JESSICA   Well, I'll set you forth.
                              ⌜*They*⌝ *exit.*

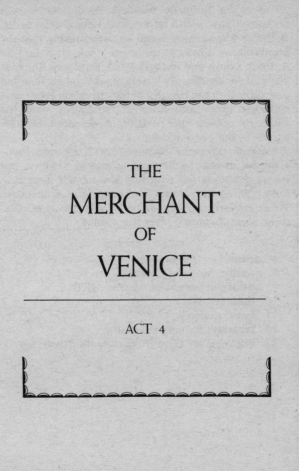

THE
MERCHANT
OF
VENICE

ACT 4

4.1 In court at Venice, Shylock demands that the terms of his bond be fulfilled. Portia enters as a doctor of laws, with a letter of introduction from Dr. Bellario. She saves Antonio by determining that the bond allows Shylock no more than a pound of Antonio's flesh and not a drop of his blood. She also finds Shylock guilty of plotting the death of a Venetian and subject to the penalty of forfeiting his estate and suffering execution. Antonio intercedes with the Duke to reduce the penalty. A defeated Shylock agrees to the proposed terms.

Bassanio offers the disguised Portia the three thousand ducats that he brought to give to Shylock, but Portia demands the ring that she herself gave Bassanio. When he refuses, she departs as if insulted. When Antonio asks Bassanio to give the ring, Bassanio sends Gratiano after her with it.

---

6. **dram:** i.e., tiny amount
8. **qualify:** moderate, limit
9. **obdurate:** accent on second syllable
10. **that:** i.e., since
11. **envy:** malice
14. **tyranny:** unmerciful action
17. **our:** i.e., my (The Duke uses the royal "we.")

⌜ACT 4⌝

⌜Scene 1⌝
Enter the Duke, the Magnificoes, Antonio, Bassanio,
⌜*Salerio,*⌝ *and Gratiano,* ⌜*with Attendants.*⌝

DUKE What, is Antonio here?
ANTONIO Ready, so please your Grace.
DUKE
  I am sorry for thee. Thou art come to answer
  A stony adversary, an inhuman wretch,
  Uncapable of pity, void and empty   5
  From any dram of mercy.
ANTONIO   I have heard
  Your Grace hath ta'en great pains to qualify
  His rigorous course; but since he stands obdurate,
  And that no lawful means can carry me   10
  Out of his envy's reach, I do oppose
  My patience to his fury, and am armed
  To suffer with a quietness of spirit
  The very tyranny and rage of his.
DUKE
  Go, one, and call the Jew into the court.   15
SALERIO
  He is ready at the door. He comes, my lord.

Enter Shylock.

DUKE
  Make room, and let him stand before our face.—

141

19. **but . . . fashion:** only keep up this pretense

20. **the last . . . act:** i.e., the moment of performing the act itself

21. **remorse:** pity; **strange:** striking

22. **strange:** exceptional; **apparent:** obvious, visible

23. **where:** i.e., whereas

25. **loose:** relinquish

27. **moi'ty:** portion

29. **of late:** lately, recently

30. **Enow:** enough

31. **of his state:** upon his condition

33. **Tartars:** Tatars, members of Mongolian tribes

34. **offices . . . courtesy:** duties of kindness

36. **possessed:** informed; **purpose:** intend

38. **due and forfeit of:** i.e., penalty that is due according to

39–40. **the danger . . . freedom:** See note on 3.3.29–34 above.

42. **carrion:** dead, decaying

44. **humor:** whim

47. **baned:** exterminated

48. **gaping:** i.e., perhaps roasted, served with its mouth opened

50. **bagpipe . . . nose:** a reference to the nasal sound of bagpipes

51. **affection:** feeling of attraction or repulsion

52. **it:** i.e., passion

Shylock, the world thinks, and I think so too,
That thou but leadest this fashion of thy malice
To the last hour of act, and then, 'tis thought,   20
Thou'lt show thy mercy and remorse more strange
Than is thy strange apparent cruelty;
And where thou now exacts the penalty,
Which is a pound of this poor merchant's flesh,
Thou wilt not only loose the forfeiture,   25
But, touched with humane gentleness and love,
Forgive a moi'ty of the principal,
Glancing an eye of pity on his losses
That have of late so huddled on his back,
Enow to press a royal merchant down   30
And pluck commiseration of ⌐his state⌐
From brassy bosoms and rough hearts of ⌐flint,⌐
From stubborn Turks, and Tartars never trained
To offices of tender courtesy.
We all expect a gentle answer, Jew.   35

SHYLOCK
I have possessed your Grace of what I purpose,
And by our holy Sabbath have I sworn
To have the due and forfeit of my bond.
If you deny it, let the danger light
Upon your charter and your city's freedom!   40
You'll ask me why I rather choose to have
A weight of carrion flesh than to receive
Three thousand ducats. I'll not answer that,
But say it is my humor. Is it answered?
What if my house be troubled with a rat,   45
And I be pleased to give ten thousand ducats
To have it baned? What, are you answered yet?
Some men there are love not a gaping pig,
Some that are mad if they behold a cat,
And others, when the bagpipe sings i' th' nose,   50
Cannot contain their urine; for affection
Masters ⌐oft⌐ passion, sways it to the mood

55, 56, 57. **he:** one man . . . another, . . . another
57. **of force:** necessarily
61. **lodged:** settled; **certain:** fixed, resolved
62. **follow:** pursue
63. **losing:** unprofitable
65. **current:** course
66. **bound:** obliged
71. **question:** dispute
73. **main flood:** ocean; **bate:** reduce
74. **use question with:** i.e., ask
78. **fretten:** fretted, agitated

Of what it likes or loathes. Now for your answer:
As there is no firm reason to be rendered
Why he cannot abide a gaping pig,   55
Why he a harmless necessary cat,
Why he a woolen bagpipe, but of force
Must yield to such inevitable shame
As to offend, himself being offended,
So can I give no reason, nor I will not,   60
More than a lodged hate and a certain loathing
I bear Antonio, that I follow thus
A losing suit against him. Are you answered?

BASSANIO
This is no answer, thou unfeeling man,
To excuse the current of thy cruelty.   65

SHYLOCK
I am not bound to please thee with my answers.

BASSANIO
Do all men kill the things they do not love?

SHYLOCK
Hates any man the thing he would not kill?

BASSANIO
Every offence is not a hate at first.

SHYLOCK
What, wouldst thou have a serpent sting thee twice?   70

ANTONIO
I pray you, think you question with the Jew.
You may as well go stand upon the beach
And bid the main flood bate his usual height;
You may as well use question with the wolf
Why he hath made the ewe ⌜bleat⌝ for the lamb;   75
You may as well forbid the mountain pines
To wag their high tops and to make no noise
When they are fretten with the gusts of heaven;
You may as well do anything most hard
As seek to soften that than which what's harder?—   80
His Jewish heart. Therefore I do beseech you

83. **conveniency:** fitness, proper action
88. **draw:** accept
93. **parts:** duties
101. **dearly:** expensively.
104. **stand for:** i.e., uphold, stand up for
105. **Upon:** according to
107. **determine:** decide
109. **stays without:** waits outside
111. **New:** i.e., newly

Make no more offers, use no farther means,
But with all brief and plain conveniency
Let me have judgment and the Jew his will.

BASSANIO
For thy three thousand ducats here is six.   85

SHYLOCK
If every ducat in six thousand ducats
Were in six parts, and every part a ducat,
I would not draw them. I would have my bond.

DUKE
How shalt thou hope for mercy, rend'ring none?

SHYLOCK
What judgment shall I dread, doing no wrong?   90
You have among you many a purchased slave,
Which, like your asses and your dogs and mules,
You use in abject and in slavish parts
Because you bought them. Shall I say to you
"Let them be free! Marry them to your heirs!   95
Why sweat they under burdens? Let their beds
Be made as soft as yours, and let their palates
Be seasoned with such viands"? You will answer
"The slaves are ours!" So do I answer you:
The pound of flesh which I demand of him   100
Is dearly bought; ⌐'tis⌐ mine and I will have it.
If you deny me, fie upon your law:
There is no force in the decrees of Venice.
I stand for judgment. Answer: shall I have it?

DUKE
Upon my power I may dismiss this court   105
Unless Bellario, a learnèd doctor
Whom I have sent for to determine this,
Come here today.

SALERIO   My lord, here stays without
A messenger with letters from the doctor,   110
New come from Padua.

116. **tainted:** infected; **wether:** male sheep, ram (usually a neutered ram)

117. **Meetest:** most suitable

120. **live still:** continue to live

127. **hangman:** state executioner; **keenness:** (1) sharpness; (2) fierceness

128. **envy:** malice

129. **wit:** intelligence

130. **inexecrable:** perhaps, an intensified form of "execrable," abhorrent (or perhaps a misprint for "inexorable")

133. **hold opinion:** agree; **Pythagoras:** ancient Greek philosopher who taught the transmigration of souls (as described in lines 134–35)

DUKE
Bring us the letters. Call the messenger.

BASSANIO
Good cheer, Antonio! What, man, courage yet!
The Jew shall have my flesh, blood, bones, and all
Ere thou shalt lose for me one drop of blood!   115

ANTONIO
I am a tainted wether of the flock,
Meetest for death. The weakest kind of fruit
Drops earliest to the ground, and so let me.
You cannot better be employed, Bassanio,
Than to live still and write mine epitaph.   120

Enter Nerissa, ⌈disguised as a lawyer's clerk.⌉

DUKE
Came you from Padua, from Bellario?

NERISSA
From both, my lord. Bellario greets your Grace.
  ⌈*Handing him a paper, which he reads, aside, while
  Shylock sharpens his knife on the sole of his shoe.*⌉

BASSANIO
Why dost thou whet thy knife so earnestly?

SHYLOCK
To cut the forfeiture from that bankrout there.

GRATIANO
Not on thy sole but on thy soul, harsh Jew,   125
Thou mak'st thy knife keen. But no metal can,
No, not the hangman's axe, bear half the keenness
Of thy sharp envy. Can no prayers pierce thee?

SHYLOCK
No, none that thou hast wit enough to make.

GRATIANO
O, be thou damned, inexecrable dog,   130
And for thy life let justice be accused;
Thou almost mak'st me waver in my faith,
To hold opinion with Pythagoras

136. **Governed:** i.e., inhabited

137. **fell:** cruel, pitiless; **fleet:** pass out of the body

138. **unhallowed:** unholy; **dam:** mother (term usually reserved for animals)

141. **rail:** revile, taunt abusively

142. **but offend'st:** only damage

145. **commend:** i.e., recommend

148. **hard by:** nearby

151. **give . . . conduct:** i.e., courteously conduct him

153. **the receipt:** i.e., the moment of receiving

156. **doctor:** i.e., doctor of laws, learned person

158. **turned o'er:** searched

159. **furnished:** provided

159–60. **opinion:** judgment

162. **fill up:** fulfill

163. **stead:** place; **lack of years:** youth

164. **let him lack:** cause him to lack; **reverend estimation:** high esteem

That souls of animals infuse themselves
Into the trunks of men. Thy currish spirit   135
Governed a wolf who, hanged for human slaughter,
Even from the gallows did his fell soul fleet,
And whilst thou layest in thy unhallowed dam,
Infused itself in thee, for thy desires
Are wolfish, bloody, starved, and ravenous.   140

SHYLOCK
Till thou canst rail the seal from off my bond,
Thou but offend'st thy lungs to speak so loud.
Repair thy wit, good youth, or it will fall
To cureless ruin. I stand here for law.

DUKE
This letter from Bellario doth commend   145
A young and learnèd doctor to our court.
Where is he?

NERISSA   He attendeth here hard by
To know your answer whether you'll admit him.

DUKE
With all my heart.—Some three or four of you   150
Go give him courteous conduct to this place.
⌜*Attendants exit.*⌝
Meantime the court shall hear Bellario's letter.
⌜*He reads.*⌝

*Your Grace shall understand that, at the receipt of
your letter, I am very sick, but in the instant that your
messenger came, in loving visitation was with me a*   155
*young doctor of Rome. His name is Balthazar. I
acquainted him with the cause in controversy between
the Jew and Antonio the merchant. We turned o'er
many books together. He is furnished with my opin-
ion, which, bettered with his own learning (the great-*   160
*ness whereof I cannot enough commend), comes with
him at my importunity to fill up your Grace's request
in my stead. I beseech you let his lack of years be no
impediment to let him lack a reverend estimation, for I*

166. **trial:** performance when put to the test

167. **publish:** make known

168. **You hear . . . writes:** i.e., you hear what the learned Bellario writes

173. **difference:** dispute

174. **holds . . . question:** i.e., is now being considered

175. **throughly:** i.e., thoroughly

181. **in such rule:** i.e., in such strict accord with the law

183. **danger:** power

186. **confess:** acknowledge

never knew so young a body with so old a head. I   165
leave him to your gracious acceptance, whose trial
shall better publish his commendation.

You hear the learnèd Bellario what he writes.

*Enter Portia for Balthazar, ⌈disguised as a lawyer, with
Attendants.⌉*

And here I take it is the doctor come.—
Give me your hand. Come you from old Bellario?   170

PORTIA
I did, my lord.

DUKE   You are welcome. Take your place.
Are you acquainted with the difference
That holds this present question in the court?

PORTIA
I am informèd throughly of the cause.   175
Which is the merchant here? And which the Jew?

DUKE
Antonio and old Shylock, both stand forth.

PORTIA
Is your name Shylock?

SHYLOCK   Shylock is my name.

PORTIA
Of a strange nature is the suit you follow,   180
Yet in such rule that the Venetian law
Cannot impugn you as you do proceed.
⌈*To Antonio.*⌉ You stand within his danger, do you
not?

ANTONIO
Ay, so he says.   185

PORTIA   Do you confess the bond?

ANTONIO
I do.

PORTIA   Then must the Jew be merciful.

SHYLOCK
On what compulsion must I? Tell me that.

190. **strained:** constrained, compelled

192. **is twice blest:** i.e., gives a double blessing

194. **becomes:** adorns

197. **attribute to:** i.e., symbol of

199. **sway:** power

200. **It:** i.e., mercy

204. **plea:** suit

205–6. **none . . . salvation:** According to Christian doctrine, because of Adam and Eve's fall into sin, only God's mercy can provide salvation.

206. **We . . . mercy:** According to the Lord's Prayer (in the New Testament), we are to ask God to forgive us "as we forgive those who trespass against us."

209. **To mitigate the justice:** i.e., to temper with mercy the strict justice

213. **My . . . head:** i.e., I bear responsibility for what I do

214. **penalty . . . bond:** i.e., the penalty prescribed in the bond if the payment is forfeited

216. **tender:** offer

219. **On forfeit of:** i.e., if I fail to pay, I agree to forfeit

PORTIA
The quality of mercy is not strained.   190
It droppeth as the gentle rain from heaven
Upon the place beneath. It is twice blest:
It blesseth him that gives and him that takes.
'Tis mightiest in the mightiest; it becomes
The thronèd monarch better than his crown.   195
His scepter shows the force of temporal power,
The attribute to awe and majesty
Wherein doth sit the dread and fear of kings;
But mercy is above this sceptered sway.
It is enthronèd in the hearts of kings;   200
It is an attribute to God Himself;
And earthly power doth then show likest God's
When mercy seasons justice. Therefore, Jew,
Though justice be thy plea, consider this:
That in the course of justice none of us   205
Should see salvation. We do pray for mercy,
And that same prayer doth teach us all to render
The deeds of mercy. I have spoke thus much
To mitigate the justice of thy plea,
Which, if thou follow, this strict court of Venice   210
Must needs give sentence 'gainst the merchant
     there.
SHYLOCK
My deeds upon my head! I crave the law,
The penalty and forfeit of my bond.
PORTIA
Is he not able to discharge the money?   215
BASSANIO
Yes. Here I tender it for him in the court,
Yea, twice the sum. If that will not suffice,
I will be bound to pay it ten times o'er
On forfeit of my hands, my head, my heart.
If this will not suffice, it must appear   220

221. **bears down:** oppresses

223. **Wrest . . . authority:** i.e., just this once use your power to bend the law

231. **Daniel:** In the story of Susanna and the Elders found in the biblical Apocrypha, the young Daniel judged the elders who spied on and accused Susanna. His wisdom saved her from death.

244. **tenor:** actual wording

That malice bears down truth. ⌜*To the Duke.*⌝ And I
  beseech you,
Wrest once the law to your authority.
To do a great right, do a little wrong,
And curb this cruel devil of his will.   225

PORTIA
It must not be. There is no power in Venice
Can alter a decree establishèd;
'Twill be recorded for a precedent
And many an error by the same example
Will rush into the state. It cannot be.   230

SHYLOCK
A Daniel come to judgment! Yea, a Daniel.
O wise young judge, how I do honor thee!

PORTIA
I pray you let me look upon the bond.

SHYLOCK
Here 'tis, most reverend doctor, here it is.
                ⌜*Handing Portia a paper.*⌝

PORTIA
Shylock, there's thrice thy money offered thee.   235

SHYLOCK
An oath, an oath, I have an oath in heaven!
Shall I lay perjury upon my soul?
⌜No,⌝ not for Venice!

PORTIA   Why, this bond is forfeit,
And lawfully by this the Jew may claim   240
A pound of flesh, to be by him cut off
Nearest the merchant's heart.—Be merciful;
Take thrice thy money; bid me tear the bond.

SHYLOCK
When it is paid according to the tenor.
It doth appear you are a worthy judge;   245
You know the law; your exposition
Hath been most sound. I charge you by the law,
Whereof you are a well-deserving pillar,

251. **stay . . . bond:** i.e., await the fulfillment of the terms in my bond

258. **Hath full relation to:** i.e., fully authorize

267. **balance:** scales (a beam with weighing pans at each side)

269. **Have . . . charge:** i.e., have in attendance at your expense   **surgeon:** a man (usually not a university-educated physician) trained and licensed to perform surgery

270. **stop:** stanch

271. **nominated:** named, specified

272. **so expressed:** i.e., made explicit

274. **it:** i.e., the requirement to provide a surgeon

Proceed to judgment. By my soul I swear
There is no power in the tongue of man   250
To alter me. I stay here on my bond.

ANTONIO
Most heartily I do beseech the court
To give the judgment.

PORTIA   Why, then, thus it is:
You must prepare your bosom for his knife—   255

SHYLOCK
O noble judge! O excellent young man!

PORTIA
For the intent and purpose of the law
Hath full relation to the penalty,
Which here appeareth due upon the bond.

SHYLOCK
'Tis very true. O wise and upright judge,   260
How much more elder art thou than thy looks!

PORTIA, ⌜to Antonio⌝
Therefore lay bare your bosom—

SHYLOCK   Ay, his breast!
So says the bond, doth it not, noble judge?
"Nearest his heart." Those are the very words.   265

PORTIA
It is so.
Are there balance here to weigh the flesh?

SHYLOCK   I have them ready.

PORTIA
Have by some surgeon, Shylock, on your charge,
To stop his wounds, lest he do bleed to death.   270

SHYLOCK
Is it so nominated in the bond?

PORTIA
It is not so expressed, but what of that?
'Twere good you do so much for charity.

SHYLOCK
I cannot find it. 'Tis not in the bond.

280. **Than is her custom:** i.e., than she usually does; **still her use:** always her habit

283. **age:** old age

284. **cut me off:** separate me (with a pun on the normal meaning of "cut off")

286. **process:** story; manner

287. **speak me fair:** i.e., speak well of me

289. **had not once a love:** i.e., did not once have someone who loved him

290. **Repent but you that:** regret only that

291. **repents not:** does not regret

295. **Which:** i.e., who

PORTIA
  You, merchant, have you anything to say?   275
ANTONIO
  But little. I am armed and well prepared.—
  Give me your hand, Bassanio. Fare you well.
  Grieve not that I am fall'n to this for you,
  For herein Fortune shows herself more kind
  Than is her custom: it is still her use   280
  To let the wretched man outlive his wealth,
  To view with hollow eye and wrinkled brow
  An age of poverty, from which ling'ring penance
  Of such misery doth she cut me off.
  Commend me to your honorable wife,   285
  Tell her the process of Antonio's end,
  Say how I loved you, speak me fair in death,
  And when the tale is told, bid her be judge
  Whether Bassanio had not once a love.
  Repent but you that you shall lose your friend   290
  And he repents not that he pays your debt.
  For if the Jew do cut but deep enough,
  I'll pay it instantly with all my heart.
BASSANIO
  Antonio, I am married to a wife
  Which is as dear to me as life itself,   295
  But life itself, my wife, and all the world
  Are not with me esteemed above thy life.
  I would lose all, ay, sacrifice them all
  Here to this devil, to deliver you.
PORTIA
  Your wife would give you little thanks for that   300
  If she were by to hear you make the offer.
GRATIANO
  I have a wife who I protest I love.
  I would she were in heaven, so she could
  Entreat some power to change this currish Jew.

306. **make else:** i.e., otherwise make

309. **Would:** i.e., I wish; **Barabbas:** a thief set free when Jesus was condemned to death

311. **trifle time:** i.e., trifle with time, waste time

319. **no jot of blood:** i.e., no blood at all

324. **confiscate:** i.e., confiscated

328. **act:** decree, law

NERISSA
'Tis well you offer it behind her back.   305
The wish would make else an unquiet house.

SHYLOCK
These be the Christian husbands! I have a
    daughter—
Would any of the stock of Barabbas
Had been her husband, rather than a Christian!   310
We trifle time. I pray thee, pursue sentence.

PORTIA
A pound of that same merchant's flesh is thine:
The court awards it, and the law doth give it.

SHYLOCK   Most rightful judge!

PORTIA
And you must cut this flesh from off his breast: 315
The law allows it, and the court awards it.

SHYLOCK
Most learnèd judge! A sentence! Come, prepare.

PORTIA
Tarry a little. There is something else.
This bond doth give thee here no jot of blood.
The words expressly are "a pound of flesh."   320
Take then thy bond, take thou thy pound of flesh,
But in the cutting it, if thou dost shed
One drop of Christian blood, thy lands and goods
Are by the laws of Venice confiscate
Unto the state of Venice.   325

GRATIANO
O upright judge!—Mark, Jew.—O learnèd judge!

SHYLOCK
Is that the law?

PORTIA   Thyself shalt see the act.
For, as thou urgest justice, be assured
Thou shalt have justice more than thou desir'st.   330

GRATIANO
O learnèd judge!—Mark, Jew, a learnèd judge!

335. **Soft:** i.e., wait a moment; **all justice:** i.e., only justice

341. **a just pound:** i.e., exactly a pound; **it:** i.e., the surplus or deficiency

342. **substance:** mass, matter

343. **division:** fraction

344. **scruple:** the twenty-fourth part of an ounce (The twentieth part of a scruple was a "grain.")

345. **But in the estimation:** i.e., even so much as

348. **I . . . hip:** i.e., I have the advantage over you (a wrestling term)

356. **barely:** merely

SHYLOCK
  I take this offer then. Pay the bond thrice
  And let the Christian go.
BASSANIO   Here is the money.
PORTIA
  Soft! The Jew shall have all justice. Soft, no haste!   335
  He shall have nothing but the penalty.
GRATIANO
  O Jew, an upright judge, a learnèd judge!
PORTIA
  Therefore prepare thee to cut off the flesh.
  Shed thou no blood, nor cut thou less nor more
  But just a pound of flesh. If thou tak'st more   340
  Or less than a just pound, be it but so much
  As makes it light or heavy in the substance
  Or the division of the twentieth part
  Of one poor scruple—nay, if the scale do turn
  But in the estimation of a hair,   345
  Thou diest, and all thy goods are confiscate.
GRATIANO
  A second Daniel! A Daniel, Jew!
  Now, infidel, I have you on the hip.
PORTIA
  Why doth the Jew pause? Take thy forfeiture.
SHYLOCK
  Give me my principal and let me go.   350
BASSANIO
  I have it ready for thee. Here it is
PORTIA
  He hath refused it in the open court.
  He shall have merely justice and his bond.
GRATIANO
  A Daniel still, say I! A second Daniel!—
  I thank thee, Jew, for teaching me that word.   355
SHYLOCK
  Shall I not have barely my principal?

360. **I'll . . . question:** i.e., I'll wait for no further disputation

364. **an alien:** As a Jew, Shylock would have been denied citizenship in Venice.

369. **privy coffer:** private account

371. **'gainst . . . voice:** i.e., without appeal

372. **predicament:** situation, condition

377. **rehearsed:** described

379. **leave:** permission

383. **charge:** expense

386. **For:** i.e., as for

388. **humbleness:** i.e., a proper attitude of humility and abjectness; **drive unto:** reduce to

PORTIA
　Thou shalt have nothing but the forfeiture
　To be so taken at thy peril, Jew.
SHYLOCK
　Why, then, the devil give him good of it!
　I'll stay no longer question.　⌈*He begins to exit.*⌉ 360
PORTIA　　　　　　　　　　　Tarry, Jew.
　The law hath yet another hold on you.
　It is enacted in the laws of Venice,
　If it be proved against an alien
　That by direct or indirect attempts　　　　　　　365
　He seek the life of any citizen,
　The party 'gainst the which he doth contrive
　Shall seize one half his goods; the other half
　Comes to the privy coffer of the state,
　And the offender's life lies in the mercy　　　　370
　Of the Duke only, 'gainst all other voice.
　In which predicament I say thou stand'st,
　For it appears by manifest proceeding
　That indirectly, and directly too,
　Thou hast contrived against the very life　　　　375
　Of the defendant, and thou hast incurred
　The danger formerly by me rehearsed.
　Down, therefore, and beg mercy of the Duke.
GRATIANO
　Beg that thou mayst have leave to hang thyself!
　And yet, thy wealth being forfeit to the state,　380
　Thou hast not left the value of a cord;
　Therefore thou must be hanged at the state's
　　charge.
DUKE
　That thou shalt see the difference of our spirit,
　I pardon thee thy life before thou ask it.　　　　385
　For half thy wealth, it is Antonio's;
　The other half comes to the general state,
　Which humbleness may drive unto a fine.

389. **Ay . . . Antonio:** i.e., the state's claim may be reduced to a fine, but not Antonio's claim to the other half

395. **halter gratis:** hangman's rope free of charge

397. **quit:** set aside

398. **so:** i.e., provided that

399. **in use:** i.e., in trust

403. **presently:** immediately

405. **of all . . . possessed:** i.e., of all that he owns at the time of his death

406. **son:** i.e., son-in-law

411. **draw:** i.e., draw up

PORTIA
　Ay, for the state, not for Antonio.
SHYLOCK
　Nay, take my life and all. Pardon not that.　　　　390
　You take my house when you do take the prop
　That doth sustain my house; you take my life
　When you do take the means whereby I live.
PORTIA
　What mercy can you render him, Antonio?
GRATIANO
　A halter gratis, nothing else, for God's sake!　　　395
ANTONIO
　So please my lord the Duke and all the court
　To quit the fine for one half of his goods,
　I am content, so he will let me have
　The other half in use, to render it
　Upon his death unto the gentleman　　　　　　400
　That lately stole his daughter.
　Two things provided more: that for this favor
　He presently become a Christian;
　The other, that he do record a gift,
　Here in the court, of all he dies possessed　　　405
　Unto his son Lorenzo and his daughter.
DUKE
　He shall do this, or else I do recant
　The pardon that I late pronouncèd here.
PORTIA
　Art thou contented, Jew? What dost thou say?
SHYLOCK
　I am content.　　　　　　　　　　　　　410
PORTIA　　　　　Clerk, draw a deed of gift.
SHYLOCK
　I pray you give me leave to go from hence.
　I am not well. Send the deed after me
　And I will sign it.
DUKE　　　　　Get thee gone, but do it.　　　415

417. **ten more:** Twelve is the number in a jury, which, according to Gratiano, should have sentenced Shylock to death.

419. **home:** i.e., to come home

422. **meet:** fitting

424. **gratify:** reward

425. **bound:** obligated

430. **cope . . . withal:** i.e., give you in exchange for your kind efforts

437. **know me . . . again:** a polite phrase meaning that one person has been introduced to the other (with a secondary, hidden meaning: "Recognize me")

439. **of force:** necessarily; **attempt you further:** i.e., again try to offer you something

⌜GRATIANO⌝
    In christ'ning shalt thou have two godfathers.
    Had I been judge, thou shouldst have had ten more,
    To bring thee to the gallows, not to the font.
                             ⌜*Shylock*⌝ *exits.*

DUKE, ⌜*to Portia*⌝
    Sir, I entreat you home with me to dinner.

PORTIA
    I humbly do desire your Grace of pardon.   420
    I must away this night toward Padua,
    And it is meet I presently set forth.

DUKE
    I am sorry that your leisure serves you not.—
    Antonio, gratify this gentleman,
    For in my mind you are much bound to him.   425
                  The Duke and his train exit.

BASSANIO, ⌜*to Portia*⌝
    Most worthy gentleman, I and my friend
    Have by your wisdom been this day acquitted
    Of grievous penalties, in lieu whereof
    Three thousand ducats due unto the Jew
    We freely cope your courteous pains withal.   430

ANTONIO
    And stand indebted, over and above,
    In love and service to you evermore.

PORTIA
    He is well paid that is well satisfied,
    And I, delivering you, am satisfied,
    And therein do account myself well paid.   435
    My mind was never yet more mercenary.
    I pray you know me when we meet again.
    I wish you well, and so I take my leave.
                    ⌜*She begins to exit.*⌝

BASSANIO
    Dear sir, of force I must attempt you further.
    Take some remembrance of us as a tribute,   440

445. **for your love:** i.e., as a remembrance of your love, a polite formula (But all Portia's words to Bassanio have meanings that exceed what he understands "Balthazar" to say.)

451. **have a mind:** am strongly inclined

452. **There's . . . value:** i.e., there's more to this ring than its monetary value

453. **dearest:** most expensive

456. **liberal:** generous

Not as fee. Grant me two things, I pray you:
Not to deny me, and to pardon me.

PORTIA
You press me far, and therefore I will yield.
Give me your gloves; I'll wear them for your sake—
And for your love I'll take this ring from you.   445
Do not draw back your hand; I'll take no more,
And you in love shall not deny me this.

BASSANIO
This ring, good sir? Alas, it is a trifle.
I will not shame myself to give you this.

PORTIA
I will have nothing else but only this.   450
And now methinks I have a mind to it.

BASSANIO
There's more depends on this than on the value.
The dearest ring in Venice will I give you,
And find it out by proclamation.
Only for this, I pray you pardon me.   455

PORTIA
I see, sir, you are liberal in offers.
You taught me first to beg, and now methinks
You teach me how a beggar should be answered.

BASSANIO
Good sir, this ring was given me by my wife,
And when she put it on, she made me vow   460
That I should neither sell, nor give nor lose it.

PORTIA
That 'scuse serves many men to save their gifts.
And if your wife be not a madwoman,
And know how well I have deserved this ring,
She would not hold out enemy forever   465
For giving it to me. Well, peace be with you.
                        ⌜*Portia and Nerissa*⌝ *exit.*

ANTONIO
My Lord Bassanio, let him have the ring.

468. **withal:** in addition

4.2 Gratiano gives the disguised Portia Bassanio's ring. Nerissa decides to try to obtain from Gratiano the ring that she gave to him.

———————

5. **well welcome:** most welcome
6. **you are well o'erta'en:** i.e., it's to your advantage that I've caught up to you
7. **upon more advice:** after further thought
10. **That cannot be:** i.e., I cannot have dinner with him
13. **my youth:** my boy (Nerissa)

"Phoebus' fire." (2.1.5)
From Willichius Westhovius, *Emblemata . . .* (1640).

Let his deservings and my love withal
Be valued 'gainst your wife's commandment.

BASSANIO
Go, Gratiano, run and overtake him.   470
Give him the ring, and bring him if thou canst
Unto Antonio's house. Away, make haste.

Gratiano exits.

Come, you and I will thither presently,
And in the morning early will we both
Fly toward Belmont. Come, Antonio.   475

They exit.

⌜Scene 2⌝
Enter ⌜Portia and⌝ Nerissa, ⌜still in disguise.⌝

PORTIA
Inquire the Jew's house out; give him this deed
And let him sign it. ⌜*She gives Nerissa a paper.*⌝ We'll
    away tonight,
And be a day before our husbands home.
This deed will be well welcome to Lorenzo.   5

Enter Gratiano.

GRATIANO
Fair sir, you are well o'erta'en.
My Lord Bassanio, upon more advice,
Hath sent you here this ring, and doth entreat
Your company at dinner.   ⌜*He gives her a ring.*⌝

PORTIA   That cannot be.   10
His ring I do accept most thankfully,
And so I pray you tell him. Furthermore,
I pray you show my youth old Shylock's house.

GRATIANO
That will I do.

19. **old:** i.e., lots of
21. **outface:** (1) defy; (2) lie boldly to

NERISSA   Sir, I would speak with you.   15
⌜*Aside to Portia.*⌝ I'll see if I can get my husband's
    ring,
Which I did make him swear to keep forever.
PORTIA, ⌜*aside to Nerissa*⌝
Thou mayst, I warrant! We shall have old swearing
That they did give the rings away to men;   20
But we'll outface them, and outswear them, too.—
Away, make haste! Thou know'st where I will tarry.
                                          ⌜*She exits.*⌝
NERISSA
Come, good sir, will you show me to this house?
                                          ⌜*They exit.*⌝

THE
MERCHANT
OF
VENICE

ACT 5

5.1 Portia and Nerissa return to Belmont. When Bassanio and Gratiano also return, bringing Antonio with them, Portia and Nerissa "discover" that their husbands have given away their rings. Antonio steps in and pleads with Portia to forgive Bassanio. At this request, the women return the rings to their husbands and reveal that Portia was the lawyer who saved Antonio. Portia also tells Antonio that three of his ships have successfully returned and tells Lorenzo that he is Shylock's heir.

1–17. In . . . Aeson: These lines allude to four famous love stories with very unhappy endings. In lines 18–28, Jessica and Lorenzo jokingly place their story among these famous tales.

4. Troilus: Son of King Priam of Troy, Troilus was betrayed by his lover Cressida after she was moved to the Greek camp.

8. Thisbe: In love with Pyramus, the son of an enemy family, Thisbe agreed to meet him at night but was frightened from the rendezvous by a lion. Pyramus, thinking that the lion had killed Thisbe, killed himself, as did Thisbe when she found Pyramus dead.

12. Dido: Dido, queen of Carthage, loved Aeneas, who abandoned her. (See page 196.)

13. waft: beckoned (with the willow branch, a symbol of forsaken love)

16. Medea: Because of her love for Jason, Medea used magic to restore to youth his father, Aeson. Jason later betrayed her, and in revenge she murdered their children.

19. steal from: (1) run away from; (2) rob ·

20. unthrift love: i.e., a love with no regard for wealth; or, unthrifty, prodigal lover

⌜ACT 5⌝

⌜Scene 1⌝
Enter Lorenzo and Jessica.

LORENZO
The moon shines bright. In such a night as this,
When the sweet wind did gently kiss the trees
And they did make no noise, in such a night
Troilus, methinks, mounted the Trojan walls
And sighed his soul toward the Grecian tents   5
Where Cressid lay that night.

JESSICA   In such a night
Did Thisbe fearfully o'ertrip the dew
And saw the lion's shadow ere himself
And ran dismayed away.   10

LORENZO   In such a night
Stood Dido with a willow in her hand
Upon the wild sea-banks, and waft her love
To come again to Carthage.

JESSICA   In such a night   15
Medea gathered the enchanted herbs
That did renew old Aeson.

LORENZO   In such a night
Did Jessica steal from the wealthy Jew,
And with an unthrift love did run from Venice   20
As far as Belmont.

JESSICA   In such a night
Did young Lorenzo swear he loved her well,

29. **did nobody come:** i.e., if nobody was coming
30. **footing:** i.e., footsteps
41. **but:** except
43. **nor . . . heard:** i.e., nor have we heard
45. **ceremoniously:** The welcome, rather than its preparation, will be ceremonious.
47. **Sola:** a cry that accompanied the blowing of horns during a hunt

Pyramus and Thisbe. (5.1.8)
From Ovid, *Le metamorphosi . . .* (1538).

Stealing her soul with many vows of faith,
And ne'er a true one.   25
LORENZO   In such a night
Did pretty Jessica, like a little shrew,
Slander her love, and he forgave it her.
JESSICA
I would out-night you did nobody come,
But hark, I hear the footing of a man.   30

Enter ⌜*Stephano,* ⌝ *a Messenger.*

LORENZO
Who comes so fast in silence of the night?
STEPHANO   A friend.
LORENZO
A friend? What friend? Your name, I pray you,
   friend.
STEPHANO
Stephano is my name, and I bring word   35
My mistress will before the break of day
Be here at Belmont. She doth stray about
By holy crosses, where she kneels and prays
For happy wedlock hours.
LORENZO   Who comes with her?   40
STEPHANO
None but a holy hermit and her maid.
I pray you, is my master yet returned?
LORENZO
He is not, nor we have not heard from him.—
But go we in, I pray thee, Jessica,
And ceremoniously let us prepare   45
Some welcome for the mistress of the house.

Enter ⌜*Lancelet, the* ⌝ *Clown.*

LANCELET   Sola, sola! Wo ha, ho! Sola, sola!
LORENZO   Who calls?
LANCELET   Sola! Did you see Master Lorenzo? Master
   Lorenzo, sola, sola!   50

54. **post:** messenger

57. **Let's in:** i.e., let's go in; **expect:** await

61. **music:** i.e., musical instrument, or group of musicians

65. **Become:** are appropriate to; **touches:** sounds

67. **patens:** small metal plates or disks (In the Mass, the Eucharist is placed on a gold **paten**.)

68–69. **orb . . . sings:** The stars and planets were thought to move within transparent spheres, which in turn moved in such perfect harmony with each other that they produced the music of the spheres—music that humankind could no longer hear after the fall of Adam and Eve.

70. **Still choiring:** continually singing; **young-eyed cherubins:** possibly the winged cherubs of Renaissance art; possibly the terrifyingly swift cherubim of Ezekiel 10.12, which were "full of eyes round about"

72. **muddy . . . decay:** i.e., body

74. **Diana:** another name for Cynthia, goddess of the moon

"Young-eyed cherubins." (5.1.70)
From Martin Luther, *Der zwey vnd zwentzigste Psalm . . .* (1525).

LORENZO Leave holloaing, man! Here.
LANCELET Sola! Where, where?
LORENZO Here!
LANCELET Tell him there's a post come from my mas-
    ter with his horn full of good news. My master will   55
    be here ere morning, sweet soul. ⌜*Lancelet exits.*⌝
LORENZO, ⌜*to Jessica*⌝
  Let's in, and there expect their coming.
  And yet no matter; why should we go in?—
  My friend ⌜Stephano,⌝ signify, I pray you,
  Within the house, your mistress is at hand,   60
  And bring your music forth into the air.
                         ⌜*Stephano exits.*⌝
  How sweet the moonlight sleeps upon this bank.
  Here will we sit and let the sounds of music
  Creep in our ears; soft stillness and the night
  Become the touches of sweet harmony.   65
  Sit, Jessica. Look how the floor of heaven
  Is thick inlaid with patens of bright gold.
  There's not the smallest orb which thou behold'st
  But in his motion like an angel sings,
  Still choiring to the young-eyed cherubins.   70
  Such harmony is in immortal souls,
  But whilst this muddy vesture of decay
  Doth grossly close it in, we cannot hear it.

    ⌜*Enter Stephano and musicians.*⌝

  Come, ho! and wake Diana with a hymn.
  With sweetest touches pierce your mistress' ear,   75
  And draw her home with music.
                    ⌜*Music plays.*⌝
JESSICA
  I am never merry when I hear sweet music.
LORENZO
  The reason is, your spirits are attentive.
  For do but note a wild and wanton herd

81. **Fetching mad bounds:** i.e., madly leaping

85. **make . . . stand:** i.e., all stand still

87–89. **the poet . . . floods:** Many poets wrote of Orpheus, the mythological musician, whose music was so enticing that it drew even inanimate objects toward him. (See page 192.) Probably **the poet** refers to Ovid (see his *Metamorphoses* X, 86ff.).

90. **naught:** nothing; **stockish:** i.e., like a stock or post

91. **his:** i.e., its

94. **stratagems, and spoils:** violent deeds and pillage

96. **affections:** inclinations; **Erebus:** a place of darkness between Earth and Hades

97. **Mark:** listen to

99. **his:** its

100. **naughty:** evil

104. **his:** i.e., the substitute's

106. **the main of waters:** i.e., the sea

108. **without respect:** i.e., except for the circumstances that attend it

Or race of youthful and unhandled colts,   80
Fetching mad bounds, bellowing and neighing loud,
Which is the hot condition of their blood,
If they but hear perchance a trumpet sound,
Or any air of music touch their ears,
You shall perceive them make a mutual stand,   85
Their savage eyes turned to a modest gaze
By the sweet power of music. Therefore the poet
Did feign that Orpheus drew trees, stones, and
      floods,
Since naught so stockish, hard, and full of rage,   90
But music for the time doth change his nature.
The man that hath no music in himself,
Nor is not moved with concord of sweet sounds,
Is fit for treasons, stratagems, and spoils;
The motions of his spirit are dull as night,   95
And his affections dark as ⌜Erebus.⌝
Let no such man be trusted. Mark the music.

Enter Portia and Nerissa.

PORTIA
  That light we see is burning in my hall.
  How far that little candle throws his beams!
  So shines a good deed in a naughty world.   100
NERISSA
  When the moon shone we did not see the candle.
PORTIA
  So doth the greater glory dim the less.
  A substitute shines brightly as a king
  Until a king be by, and then his state
  Empties itself as doth an inland brook   105
  Into the main of waters. Music, hark!
NERISSA
  It is your music, madam, of the house.
PORTIA
  Nothing is good, I see, without respect.
  Methinks it sounds much sweeter than by day.

110. **virtue:** power

112. **attended:** listened to, heard; or, accompanied

116. **by season:** by appearing at the proper time; **seasoned are:** are perfected, made fit

117. **right:** just

118. **Endymion:** in mythology, a mortal loved by the moon

126. **Which speed:** i.e., who prosper

129. **before:** in advance

"The moon sleeps with Endymion." (5.1.118)
From Michel de Marolles, *Tableaux du temple* . . . (1676).

NERISSA

Silence bestows that virtue on it, madam.   110

PORTIA

The crow doth sing as sweetly as the lark
When neither is attended, and I think
The nightingale, if she should sing by day
When every goose is cackling, would be thought
No better a musician than the wren.   115
How many things by season seasoned are
To their right praise and true perfection!
Peace—how the moon sleeps with Endymion
And would not be awaked!

⌜*Music ceases.*⌝

LORENZO   That is the voice,   120
Or I am much deceived, of Portia.

PORTIA

He knows me as the blind man knows the cuckoo,
By the bad voice.

LORENZO   Dear lady, welcome home.

PORTIA

We have been praying for our husbands' welfare,   125
Which speed we hope the better for our words.
Are they returned?

LORENZO   Madam, they are not yet,
But there is come a messenger before
To signify their coming.   130

PORTIA   Go in, Nerissa.
Give order to my servants that they take
No note at all of our being absent hence—
Nor you, Lorenzo—Jessica, nor you.

⌜*A trumpet sounds.*⌝

LORENZO

Your husband is at hand. I hear his trumpet.   135
We are no tell-tales, madam, fear you not.

PORTIA

This night methinks is but the daylight sick;

140–41. **We . . . sun:** i.e., we would have daylight at the same time as the other side of the world, provided you (Portia) walked about when the sun is absent

142. **be light:** be unchaste

143. **heavy:** sad

144. **never be Bassanio so:** i.e., may Bassanio never be sad

145. **God sort all:** i.e., may God arrange everything

148. **bound:** obligated; tied

149. **in all sense:** in every sense (of the word)

154. **scant:** limit, cut short; **breathing courtesy:** i.e., mere words of courtesy

157. **gelt:** gelded, castrated; **for my part:** from my point of view

161. **posy:** i.e., rhyming inscription

It looks a little paler. 'Tis a day
Such as the day is when the sun is hid.

Enter Bassanio, Antonio, Gratiano, and their followers.

BASSANIO
  We should hold day with the Antipodes   140
  If you would walk in absence of the sun.
PORTIA
  Let me give light, but let me not be light,
  For a light wife doth make a heavy husband,
  And never be Bassanio so for me.
  But God sort all! You are welcome home, my lord.   145
              ⌈*Gratiano and Nerissa talk aside.*⌉
BASSANIO
  I thank you, madam. Give welcome to my friend.
  This is the man, this is Antonio,
  To whom I am so infinitely bound.
PORTIA
  You should in all sense be much bound to him,
  For as I hear he was much bound for you.   150
ANTONIO
  No more than I am well acquitted of.
PORTIA
  Sir, you are very welcome to our house.
  It must appear in other ways than words;
  Therefore I scant this breathing courtesy.
GRATIANO, ⌈*to Nerissa*⌉
  By yonder moon I swear you do me wrong!   155
  In faith, I gave it to the judge's clerk.
  Would he were gelt that had it, for my part,
  Since you do take it, love, so much at heart.
PORTIA
  A quarrel ho, already! What's the matter?
GRATIANO
  About a hoop of gold, a paltry ring   160
  That she did give me, whose posy was

168. **Though:** i.e., if
169. **respective:** mindful
170. **Gave it:** i.e., gave it to; **God's:** i.e., as God's
171. **on 's:** on his
172. **an if:** i.e., if
175. **scrubbèd:** stunted
177. **prating:** talkative
189. **An 'twere:** i.e., if it were done; **mad:** upset
190. **I were best to:** i.e., I had better

Orpheus. (5.1.88)
From Ovid, *Metamorphoseon* . . . (1565).

For all the world like cutler's poetry
Upon a knife, "Love me, and leave me not."

NERISSA
What talk you of the posy or the value?
You swore to me when I did give ⌈it⌉ you   165
That you would wear it till your hour of death,
And that it should lie with you in your grave.
Though not for me, yet for your vehement oaths,
You should have been respective and have kept it.
Gave it a judge's clerk! No, God's my judge,   170
The clerk will ne'er wear hair on 's face that had it.

GRATIANO
He will, an if he live to be a man.

NERISSA
Ay, if a woman live to be a man.

GRATIANO
Now, by this hand, I gave it to a youth,
A kind of boy, a little scrubbèd boy,   175
No higher than thyself, the judge's clerk,
A prating boy that begged it as a fee.
I could not for my heart deny it him.

PORTIA
You were to blame, I must be plain with you,
To part so slightly with your wife's first gift,   180
A thing stuck on with oaths upon your finger,
And so riveted with faith unto your flesh.
I gave my love a ring and made him swear
Never to part with it, and here he stands.
I dare be sworn for him he would not leave it   185
Nor pluck it from his finger for the wealth
That the world masters. Now, in faith, Gratiano,
You give your wife too unkind a cause of grief.
An 'twere to me I should be mad at it.

BASSANIO, ⌈*aside*⌉
Why, I were best to cut my left hand off   190
And swear I lost the ring defending it.

211. **conceive:** understand
212. **left:** parted with
215. **virtue:** power
217. **contain:** retain
221. **wanted the modesty:** lacked the restraint
222. **held . . . ceremony:** kept for its symbolic value
224. **I'll . . . but:** i.e., I'll bet my life that

GRATIANO
My Lord Bassanio gave his ring away
Unto the judge that begged it, and indeed
Deserved it, too. And then the boy, his clerk,
That took some pains in writing, he begged mine,   195
And neither man nor master would take aught
But the two rings.
PORTIA   What ring gave you, my lord?
Not that, I hope, which you received of me.
BASSANIO
If I could add a lie unto a fault,   200
I would deny it, but you see my finger
Hath not the ring upon it. It is gone.
PORTIA
Even so void is your false heart of truth.
By heaven, I will ne'er come in your bed
Until I see the ring!   205
NERISSA, ⌜to Gratiano⌝ Nor I in yours
Till I again see mine!
BASSANIO   Sweet Portia,
If you did know to whom I gave the ring,
If you did know for whom I gave the ring,   210
And would conceive for what I gave the ring,
And how unwillingly I left the ring,
When naught would be accepted but the ring,
You would abate the strength of your displeasure.
PORTIA
If you had known the virtue of the ring,   215
Or half her worthiness that gave the ring,
Or your own honor to contain the ring,
You would not then have parted with the ring.
What man is there so much unreasonable,
If you had pleased to have defended it   220
With any terms of zeal, wanted the modesty
To urge the thing held as a ceremony?
Nerissa teaches me what to believe:
I'll die for 't but some woman had the ring!

226. **civil doctor:** doctor of civil law
227. **Which:** i.e., who
229. **suffered:** allowed
230. **held up:** i.e., upheld, preserved
236. **candles of the night:** stars
242. **liberal:** generous
246. **Argus:** the mythological giant with a hundred eyes, used as a round-the-clock guard
253. **mar . . . pen:** a bawdy threat

Dido. (5.1.12)
From Guillaume Rouille,
Promptuarii iconum . . . (1553).

BASSANIO
No, by my honor, madam, by my soul,   225
No woman had it, but a civil doctor,
Which did refuse three thousand ducats of me
And begged the ring, the which I did deny him
And suffered him to go displeased away,
Even he that had held up the very life   230
Of my dear friend. What should I say, sweet lady?
I was enforced to send it after him.
I was beset with shame and courtesy.
My honor would not let ingratitude
So much besmear it. Pardon me, good lady,   235
For by these blessèd candles of the night,
Had you been there, I think you would have begged
The ring of me to give the worthy doctor.

PORTIA
Let not that doctor e'er come near my house!
Since he hath got the jewel that I loved,   240
And that which you did swear to keep for me,
I will become as liberal as you:
I'll not deny him anything I have,
No, not my body, nor my husband's bed.
Know him I shall, I am well sure of it.   245
Lie not a night from home. Watch me like Argus.
If you do not, if I be left alone,
Now by mine honor, which is yet mine own,
I'll have that doctor for ⌈my⌉ bedfellow.

NERISSA
And I his clerk. Therefore be well advised   250
How you do leave me to mine own protection.

GRATIANO
Well, do you so. Let not me take him, then,
For if I do, I'll mar the young clerk's pen.

ANTONIO
I am th' unhappy subject of these quarrels.

257. **enforcèd wrong:** compulsory error

264. **oath of credit:** i.e., credible oath

268. **for his wealth:** i.e., in order to enrich him

269. **but:** except

270. **Had quite miscarried:** i.e., (my body) would have been utterly lost

271. **My soul upon:** i.e., with my soul as

272. **advisedly:** knowingly

281. **In lieu of this:** i.e., in return for this ring

PORTIA
  Sir, grieve not you. You are welcome   255
    notwithstanding.
BASSANIO
  Portia, forgive me this enforcèd wrong,
  And in the hearing of these many friends
  I swear to thee, even by thine own fair eyes,
  Wherein I see myself—   260
PORTIA   Mark you but that!
  In both my eyes he doubly sees himself,
  In each eye one. Swear by your double self,
  And there's an oath of credit.
BASSANIO   Nay, but hear me.   265
  Pardon this fault, and by my soul I swear
  I never more will break an oath with thee.
ANTONIO
  I once did lend my body for his wealth,
  Which but for him that had your husband's ring
  Had quite miscarried. I dare be bound again,   270
  My soul upon the forfeit, that your lord
  Will never more break faith advisedly.
PORTIA
  Then you shall be his surety. Give him this,
                ⌈*Giving Antonio a ring.*⌉
  And bid him keep it better than the other.
ANTONIO
  Here, Lord Bassanio, swear to keep this ring.   275
BASSANIO
  By heaven, it is the same I gave the doctor!
PORTIA
  I had it of him. Pardon me, Bassanio,
  For by this ring, the doctor lay with me.
NERISSA
  And pardon me, my gentle Gratiano,
  For that same scrubbèd boy, the doctor's clerk,   280
  In lieu of this, last night did lie with me.
                ⌈*She shows a ring.*⌉

282–83. **this . . . enough:** i.e., since, in the summer, dirt roads were easily traveled, there was no need then to repair them

285. **amazed:** bewildered

299. **dumb:** i.e., dumbstruck

306. **living:** livelihood

308. **road:** i.e., harbor

GRATIANO
Why, this is like the mending of highways
In summer, where the ways are fair enough!
What, are we cuckolds ere we have deserved it?

PORTIA
Speak not so grossly.—You are all amazed.   285
⌜*She hands a paper to Bassanio.*⌝
Here is a letter; read it at your leisure.
It comes from Padua from Bellario.
There you shall find that Portia was the doctor,
Nerissa there, her clerk. Lorenzo here
Shall witness I set forth as soon as you,   290
And even but now returned. I have not yet
Entered my house.—Antonio, you are welcome,
And I have better news in store for you
Than you expect. Unseal this letter soon.
⌜*Handing him a paper.*⌝
There you shall find three of your argosies   295
Are richly come to harbor suddenly.
You shall not know by what strange accident
I chancèd on this letter.

ANTONIO   I am dumb.

BASSANIO
Were you the doctor and I knew you not?   300

GRATIANO
Were you the clerk that is to make me cuckold?

NERISSA
Ay, but the clerk that never means to do it,
Unless he live until he be a man.

BASSANIO, ⌜*to Portia*⌝
Sweet doctor, you shall be my bedfellow.
When I am absent, then lie with my wife.   305

ANTONIO
Sweet lady, you have given me life and living;
For here I read for certain that my ships
Are safely come to road.

319. **Of:** about; **at full:** fully
320. **charge . . . inter'gatories:** i.e., oblige us to answer questions, as if in court under oath
324. **stay:** wait
329. **sore:** i.e., sorely, greatly

PORTIA   How now, Lorenzo?
My clerk hath some good comforts too for you.   310

NERISSA
Ay, and I'll give them him without a fee.
                            ⌈*Handing him a paper.*⌉
There do I give to you and Jessica,
From the rich Jew, a special deed of gift,
After his death, of all he dies possessed of.

LORENZO
Fair ladies, you drop manna in the way   315
Of starvèd people.

PORTIA   It is almost morning,
And yet I am sure you are not satisfied
Of these events at full. Let us go in,
And charge us there upon inter'gatories,   320
And we will answer all things faithfully.

GRATIANO
Let it be so. The first inter'gatory
That my Nerissa shall be sworn on is
Whether till the next night she had rather stay
Or go to bed now, being two hours to day.   325
But were the day come, I should wish it dark
Till I were couching with the doctor's clerk.
Well, while I live, I'll fear no other thing
So sore as keeping safe Nerissa's ring.
                                    They exit.

Textual Notes

The reading of the present text appears to the left of the square bracket. The earliest sources of readings not in Q1, the quarto of 1600, upon which this edition is based, are indicated as follows: **Q2** is the quarto of 1619; **F** is the Shakespeare First Folio of 1623, in which *The Merchant of Venice* is a slightly edited reprint of Q2. **Ed.** is an earlier editor of Shakespeare, from the editor of the Second Folio of 1632 to the present. No sources are given for emendations of punctuation or for correction of obvious typographical errors, such as turned letters that produce no known word. **SD** means stage direction; **SP** means speech prefix; ~ refers to a word already quoted; **corr.** refers to the corrected state; **uncorr.** refers to the uncorrected state; ˏ indicates the omission of a punctuation mark.

1.1   0. SD *Solanio*] Ed.; *Salanio* Q1, F
     28. docked] Ed.; docks Q1, F
    47, 49. SP SOLANIO] Ed.; *Sola.* Q1, F
   63, 68, 72. SP SALARINO] Ed.; *Sala.* (or *Sal.*) Q1, F
     119. tongue] togue Q1
     120. Is] Ed.; It is Q1, F
     135. off] Q1 (of)
     158. back] Q1 (bake)
1.2   55. Bon] Ed.; *Boune* Q1, F
     61. throstle] Ed.; Trassell Q1, F
     121. SD *1 line later in* Q1
1.3 29, 33, 41. SP SHYLOCK] Ed.; *Iew.* (or *Jew.*) Q1, F
     190. SD *1 line earlier in* Q1, F
2.1   26. Sophyˏ . . . prince,] Ed.; ~, . . . ~ˏ Q1, F
     32. thee] Ed.; the Q1, F
     36. page] Ed.; rage Q1, F

2.2   1. SP LANCELET] this ed.; *Clowne.* Q1, F
        98. last] Q2; lost Q1, F
        117. SD *The Attendant exits.*] Q2 (*Exit one of his men.*); *omit* Q1, F
148, 155. SP LANCELET] this ed.; *Clowne.* Q1, F
        167. SD *Lancelet and old Gobbo exit.*] this ed.; *Exit Clowne.* Q1, F
        174. SD *2 lines earlier in* Q1, F
2.3   0. SD *Lancelet Gobbo*] this ed.; *the Clowne* Q1, F
        10. SP LANCELET] this ed.; *Clowne* Q1, F
        15. SD *1 line earlier in* Q2, F
2.4   0. SD *Solanio*] Ed.; *Salanio* Q1, F
        9. SD *1 line later in* Q1, F; F *adds* "with a Letter."
        23. SD *Lancelet exits.*] Q1 *and* F *print* "Exit Clowne" *3 lines later.*
27, 31. SP SALARINO] Ed.; *Sal.* Q1, F
        28. SP SOLANIO] Ed.; *Sol.* Q1, F
2.5   0. SD *was,*] ~ ͵ Q1, F
        1. SP SHYLOCK] Ed.; *Iewe.* Q1, F
        7 *and thereafter until scene's end* SP LANCELET] *Clowne.* Q1, F
        44. Jewess'] Ed.; *Iewes* Q1, F
2.7   22. threatens. Men] ~ ͵ ~ Q1, F
        77. *tombs*] Ed.; *timber* Q1, F
2.8   41. Slubber] Q2, F; slumber Q1
2.9   51. chaff] chaft Q1
        70. *judgment*] iudement Q1
        109. Bassanio, Lord Love] Ed.; *Bassanio Lord, loue* Q1, F
3.1   0. SD *Enter*] Q2, F; *omit* Q1
        22. SD *placed as in* Q2; *1 line later in* Q1, F
        30. fledge] Q1 (fludge)
        73. SP SERVINGMAN] Ed.; *omit* Q1, F

78. SD *Salarino . . . exit.*] *Exeunt Gentlemen.*
Q1, F; Q1 *then repeats* "*Enter* Tuball."
106. heard] Ed.; heere Q1, F
120. turquoise] Ed.; Turkies Q1, F

3.2   0. SD *Enter . . . Nerissa.*] *Enter Bassanio,*
Portia, Gratiano, and all their traynes.
Q1
22. time,] ~ . Q1
63. live. With] ~ ˏ ~ Q1
71. *lies.*] ~ ˏ Q1
83. vice] Ed.; voyce Q1, F
86. stairs] Ed.; stayers Q1, F
203. loved; for] ~ ˏ ~ Q1
222. SD *2 lines later in* Q1, F

3.3   0. SD *Solanio*] F; *Salerio* Q1; *Salarino* Q2
1 *and thereafter in the scene* SP SHYLOCK]
Ed.; *Iew.* Q1, F
18. SD *He*] this ed.; *Iew.* Q1, F
19. SP SOLANIO] Ed.; *Sol.* Q1, F
27. SP SOLANIO] Ed.; *Sal.* Q1; *Sol.* F

3.4   20. soul ˏ] ~ ; Q1
23. Hear] Q1 (heere)
23. things:] ~ ˏ Q1
31. monastery] Q2, F; Monastry Q1
41, 45. fare] Q1 (far)
50. Padua] Ed.; Mantua Q1, F
51. cousin's] F; cosin Q1
55. traject] Ed.; Tranect Q1, F
58. *He exits.*] SD Q2; *omit* Q1, F
85. my whole] Q2, F; my my whole Q1

3.5   1 *and throughout scene* SP LANCELET] this
ed.; *Clowne.* Q1, F
21. e'en] Q1 (in)
27. comes] Q2, F; come Q1
63. SD *Lancelet*] this ed.; *Clowne* Q1, F

76. merit it] Ed.; meane it, it Q1, F; meane it, then Q2

84. a] F; *omit* Q1

89. howsome'er] how so mere Q1

90. digest] Q1 (disgest)

91. SD *They exit.*] F (*Exeunt.*); *Exit.* Q1

4.1

31. his state] Q2, F; this states Q1

32. flint] Q2; flints Q1, F

36 *and throughout to line* 179 SP SHYLOCK.] Ed.; *Iewe.* Q1, F

37. Sabbath] Q1 (Sabaoth)

51–52. urine; for affection / Masters oft] Ed.; vrine for affection. / Maisters of Q1, F

74. You may as] Q1 *corr.*, Q2; *omit* Q1 *uncorr.*; Or euen as F

75. Why he hath made] Q1 *corr.*; Q2; *omit* Q1 *uncorr.*, F

75. bleat] F; bleake Q1

76. mountain] F; mountaine of Q1

101. 'tis] Q2, F; as Q1

122. both, my lord. Bellario] Ed.; both? my L. *Bellario* Q1; From both. / My Lord *Bellario* F

138. whilst] Q2, F; whilest Q1

168. You] Ed.; *Duke.* You Q1, F

168. SD *1 line earlier in* Q1, F

238. No] Q2, F; Not Q1

260–317. SP SHYLOCK.] Ed.; *Iew.* Q1, F

284, 338. off] Q1 (of)

332. SP SHYLOCK.] Ed.; *Iew.* Q1, F

416. SP GRATIANO] Q2, F; *Shy.* Q1

467. Lord] Q2; L. Q1, F

469. wife's] Q1 (wiues)

4.2

0. SD *Portia and*] F; *omit* Q1

7. Lord] Q2; L. Q1, F

23. you] yov Q1
23. SD *They exit.*] F; *omit* Q1

5.1 32, 35, 41. SP STEPHANO] Ed.; *Messen.* or *Mess.*
Q1, F

47 *and thereafter throughout scene* SP LANCE-
LET] this ed.; *Clowne.* Q1, F

49. Master Lorenzo? Master Lorenzo] Ed.;
M. *Lorenzo,* & M. *Lorenzo* Q1, F

59. Stephano] Q2; *Stephen* Q1, F

64. ears; soft] ~ ʌ ~ Q1, F

76. SD *Music plays.*] Q2; *play Musique.* Q1, F

89. floods,] ~. Q1, F

96. Erebus] Ed.; *Terebus* Q1; *Erobus* F

119. SD *Music ceases.*] F; *omit* Q1

134. SD *A trumpet sounds.*] this ed.; *A Tucket
sounds.* F; *omit* Q1

165. it] Q2, F; *omit* Q1

180. wife's] Q1 (wiues)

249. my] Q2, F; mine Q1

322. inter'gatory] Q1 *corr.* (intergotory), F;
intergory Q1 *uncorr.*

The Merchant of Venice: A Modern Perspective

Alexander Leggatt

The Merchant of Venice is a comedy. Comedies traditionally end in marriage, and on the way they examine the social networks in which marriage is involved: the relations among families, among friends, among parents and children, and what in Shakespeare's society were the all-important ties of money and property. Comedies also create onstage images of closed communities of right-thinking people, from which outsiders are excluded by being laughed at. If *The Merchant of Venice* has always seemed one of Shakespeare's more problematic and disturbing comedies, this may be because it examines the networks of society more closely than usual, and treats outsiders—one in particular—with a severity that seems to go beyond the comic.

In the interweaving of the play's stories we see a chain of obligations based on money. Bassanio needs money to pay his debts, and plans to get it by marrying the rich heiress Portia. To make money he needs to borrow money—from his friend Antonio, who borrows it from Shylock, who borrows it, according to the patter of his trade, from Tubal. Once Bassanio has won Portia she becomes part of the network, and the obligations become more than financial. She imposes on herself the condition that, before her marriage is consummated, Antonio must be freed from his bond to Shylock; as she tells Bassanio, "never shall you lie by Portia's side / With an unquiet soul" (3.2.318–19). She takes on herself the task of freeing Antonio. As Bassanio must journey to

Belmont and answer the riddle of the caskets, Portia must journey to Venice and answer the riddle of Shylock's bond. Antonio thus becomes "bound" (4.1.425) to the young doctor (Portia) who saved him, and the only payment the doctor will take is Bassanio's ring. Antonio now, in effect, has to borrow from Bassanio to pay Portia: it is at Antonio's insistence that Bassanio reluctantly gives away the ring. Yet the ring represents Bassanio's tie of loyalty to Portia, the husband's obligation to be bound exclusively to his wife; she gives the ring, as Shylock gives money, with conditions attached:

> Which, when you part from, lose, or give away,
> Let it presage the ruin of your love,
> And be my vantage to exclaim on you.
> (3.2.176–78)

The line of obligation runs, like the play itself, from Venice to Belmont, then from Belmont to Venice, and back to Belmont again. The ring exemplifies the paradox of marriage: it binds two people exclusively to each other, yet it does so within a social network in which they have inevitable ties with other people, ties on which the marriage itself depends. Portia and Bassanio depend on Antonio, who is Portia's chief rival for Bassanio's affection. The story of the ring is based on paradoxes: Bassanio, in giving it to the young "doctor," is betraying Portia at her own request, and giving her back her own. In the final scene Portia gives the ring to Antonio, who returns it to Bassanio, thus participating in a symbolic exchange that cements the marriage relationship from which he is excluded. As Portia's ring comes back to Portia, then back to Bassanio, the line of obligation becomes at last a circle, the symbol at once of perfection and exclusion.

Portia is also bound to her father. When we first see

her she is chafing at the way her father has denied her freedom of choice in marriage: "So is the will of a living daughter curbed by the will of a dead father" (1.2.24–25). But by the end of that scene she is reconciled to her father's will when she hears that her unwanted suitors have departed rather than face the test; and of course Bassanio, the man she wants—the man who visited Belmont in her father's time (1.2.112–21)—is the winner. The will of the dead father and the will of the living daughter are one. Portia sees the value of the test from her own point of view when she tells Bassanio, "If you do love me, you will find me out" (3.2.43), and in the moment of victory he insists that to have satisfied her father's condition is not enough "Until confirmed, signed, ratified by you" (3.2.152). The dead father is satisfied, but theatrically the emphasis falls on the satisfaction of the living daughter.

In the story of Shylock and Jessica all these emphases are reversed. Jessica's loyalties are divided. She recognizes a real obligation to her father—"Alack, what heinous sin is it in me / To be ashamed to be my father's child" (2.3.16–17)—and she hopes her elopement will "end this strife" (2.3.20). For her it does (with reservations we will come to later); but Shakespeare puts the focus on the pain and humiliation it causes Shylock. The vicious taunts he endures from the Venetians identify him as an old man who has lost his potency, "two stones, two rich and precious stones" (2.8.20–21), and his cry, "My own flesh and blood to rebel!" draws Solanio's cruel retort, "Out upon it, old carrion! Rebels it at these years?" (3.1.35–36). While Portia's father retains his power beyond the grave, Shylock is mocked as an impotent old man. We may find Lancelet Gobbo's teasing of his blind father cruel; while Shakespeare's contemporaries had stronger stomachs for this sort of thing than we do, Shakespeare's own humor is not usually so heartless. With the taunting of Shylock he goes further: the jokes of Salarino and Solanio, like those of Iago, leave us feeling no impulse to laugh.

This brings us to the problem of the way comedy treats outsiders, and to the cruelty that so often lies at the heart of laughter. Portia begins her dissection of her unwanted suitors "I know it is a sin to be a mocker, but . . ." (1.2.57–58) and goes on to indulge that sin with real gusto. The unwanted suitors are all foreigners, and are mocked as such; only the Englishman, we notice, gets off lightly. (His fault, interestingly, is his inability to speak foreign languages; in one of the play's more complicated jokes, the insularity of the English audience, which the rest of the scene plays up to, becomes itself the target of laughter.) Morocco and Arragon lose the casket game for good reasons. Morocco chooses the gold casket because he thinks the phrase "what many men desire" is a sign of Portia's market value. This is a tribute, but not the tribute of love. Arragon thinks not of Portia's worth but of his own. Besides, Morocco and Arragon are foreign princes, and Morocco's foreignness is compounded by his dark skin, which Shakespeare emphasizes in a rare stage direction specifying the actor's costume: "*a tawny Moor all in white*" (2.1.0 SD). Portia's dismissal of him, "Let all of his complexion choose me so" (2.7.87), is for us an ugly moment. The prejudice that is, if not overturned, at least challenged and debated in *Titus Andronicus* and *Othello* is casually accepted here.

The most conspicuous problem, of course, is Shylock, and here we need to pause. *The Merchant of Venice* was written within a culture in which prejudice against Jews was pervasive and endemic. It can be argued that this goes back to the earliest days of Christianity, when the tradition began of making the Jews bear the guilt of the Crucifixion. Throughout medieval and early Renaissance Europe the prejudice bred dark fantasies: Jews were accused, for example, of conducting grotesque rituals in which they murdered Christian children and drank their blood. The story of a Jew who wants a pound of Christian flesh may have its roots in these fantasies of Jews violating Christian bodies. Shylock's profession of usury is also bound up with his race: barred from other occupations, the Jews of Europe took to money-lending. Antonio's disapproval of lending money at interest echoes traditional Christian teaching (Christian practice was another matter). Shylock's boast that he makes his gold and silver breed like ewes and rams would remind his audience of the familiar argument that usury was against the law of God because metal was sterile and could not breed. Not just in his threat to Antonio, but in his day-to-day business, Shylock would appear unnatural.

Prejudice feeds on ignorance; since the Jews had been expelled from England in 1290, Shakespeare may never have met one. (There were a few in London in his time, but they could not practice their religion openly.) Given that the villainy of Shylock is one of the mainsprings of the story, it would have been far more natural for Shakespeare to exploit this prejudice than resist it. Many critics and performers, however, have insisted that he *did* resist it. His imagination, so the argument runs, worked on the figure of Shylock until it had created sympathy for him, seeing him as the victim of persecution. The great Victorian actor Henry Irving played him as a wronged and dignified victim, representative of a suffering race. Shylock's famous self-defense, "Hath not a Jew eyes? Hath not a Jew hands . . . ?" (3.1.57–58), has been taken out of context and presented as a plea for the recognition of our common humanity. In context, however, its effect is less benevolent. Shylock's plea is compelling and eloquent, but he himself uses it not to argue for tolerance but to defend his cruelty: "The villainy you teach me I will execute, and it shall go hard but I will better the instruction" (3.1.70–72). Gratiano's taunt, "A Daniel still, say I! A second Daniel!— / I thank thee, Jew, for teaching me that word" (4.1.354–55), shows that Gratiano, along with the word "Daniel," has also picked up from Shylock, without knowing it, the word "teach," and the echo is a terrible demonstration of the ways we teach each other hate so that prejudice moves in a vicious circle.

Does the play itself break out of this circle? There is little encouragement in the text to think so. In other plays Shakespeare casually uses the word "Jew" as a term of abuse, and this usage is intensified here. The kindest thing Lorenzo's friends can find to say about Jessica is that she is "a gentle and no Jew" (2.6.53). We are aware of the pain Shylock feels in defeat; but the play emphasizes that he has brought it on himself, and no one in the play expresses sympathy for him, just as no one—except Shylock—ever questions Antonio's right to spit on him. Given the latitude of interpretation, there are ways around the problem. Critics and performers alike have found sympathy for Shylock in his suffering, and have attacked the Christians' treatment of him. But these readings are allowed rather than compelled by the text, and to a great extent they go against its surface impression.

It has to be said that many people who normally love Shakespeare find *The Merchant of Venice* painful. It even has power to do harm: it has provoked racial incidents in schools, and school boards have sometimes banned it. One may reply that the way to deal with a work one finds offensive is not censorship but criticism; in any case, everyone who teaches or performs the play needs to be aware of the problems it may create for their students and audiences, and to confront those problems as honestly as they can. At best, there are legitimate interpretations that control or resist the anti-Semitism in the text. At worst, it can be an object lesson showing that even a great writer can be bound by the prejudices of his time. To raise this kind of question is of course to go beyond the text as such and to make the problem of Shylock loom larger than it would have done for Shakespeare. In discussions of this kind, the objection "Why can't we just take it as a play?" is often heard. But we cannot place Shakespeare in a sealed container. He belonged to his time, and, as the most widely studied and performed playwright in the world, he belongs to ours. He exerts great power within our culture, and we cannot take it for granted that this power is always benevolent.

To return to the text, and to explore the ramifications of the figure of Shylock a bit further: Shylock, Morocco, and Arragon are not the play's only losers. The group, paradoxically, includes Antonio, who is the center of so much friendship and concern. In the final scene he is a loner in a world of couples, and the sadness he expressed at the beginning of the play does not really seem to have lifted. He resists attempts to make him reveal his secret; but when to Solanio's "Why then you are in love" he replies "Fie, fie!" (1.1.48) we notice it is not a direct denial. Solanio himself later makes clear the depth of Antonio's feeling for Bassanio: "I think he only loves the world for him" (2.8.52). In the trial scene Antonio tells Bassanio to report his sacrifice and bid Portia "be judge / Whether Bassanio had not once a love" (4.1.288–89). Antonio has not only accepted Bassanio's marriage; he has helped make it possible—yet there is a touch of rivalry here. In the trial his courageous acceptance of death shades into an actual yearning for it, and in the final restoration of his wealth there is something restrained and cryptic. Portia will not tell him how she came by the news that his ships have been recovered; his own response, "I am dumb" (5.1.299), has the same curtness as Shylock's "I am content" (4.1.410), and the same effect of closing off conversation. Whether we should call Antonio's love for Bassanio "homosexual" is debatable; the term did not exist until fairly recently, and some social historians argue that the concept did not exist either. Our own language of desire and love does not necessarily apply in other cultures. What matters to our understanding of the play is that Antonio's feeling for Bassanio is not only intense but leaves him excluded from the sort of happiness the other characters find as they pair off into couples. This gives Antonio an ironic affinity with his enemy Shylock: both are outsiders. Many current productions end with Antonio conspicuously alone as the couples go off to bed.

Another character who is in low spirits at the end of some productions of *The Merchant of Venice* is Jessica. There is less warrant for this in the text, apart from her line "I am never merry when I hear sweet music" (5.1.77). Jessica is a significant case of a character who has broken the barrier between outsider and insider, joining a group (the Christians) to which she did not originally belong. She is welcomed, and seems at ease in her new world, but Lancelet Gobbo, the plainspoken and sometimes anarchic clown of the play, raises doubts about the efficacy of her conversion—she is damned if she is her father's daughter, and damned if she isn't (3.5.1–25)—and about its economic consequences: "This making of Christians will raise the price of hogs" (3.5.22–23). In a play in which money counts for so much, this is a very pointed joke. Lancelet uses his clown's license to raise the question of whether Jessica will ever be fully accepted in Christian society. (His own contribution to race relations has been to get a Moor pregnant, and his reference to her does not sound affectionate.) Jessica's uneasiness at going into male disguise could suggest a worry about the deeper change she is making in her nature.

Her uneasiness also makes a revealing contrast with Portia's attitude to *her* disguise, and suggests there may be a parallel between the two women. Given her easy dominance of every scene in which she appears, it may seem odd to think of Portia as an outsider. But she is a woman in a society whose structures are male-centered and patriarchal. She greets her marriage with a surrender of herself and her property to a man who, like her father, will have full legal control over her:

> Myself, and what is mine, to you and yours
> Is now converted. But now I was the lord
> Of this fair mansion, master of my servants,
> Queen o'er myself; and even now, but now,
> This house, these servants, and this same myself
> Are yours, my lord's. (3.2.170–75)

Yet she continues to dominate Bassanio, and more than that: like Jessica, she uses male disguise to enter another world, the exclusive male club (as it then was) of the legal profession. Unlike Jessica, she moves into this new world with confidence. Her mockery of swaggering young men as she plans her disguise is irrelevant to the story but seems to answer a need in the character to poke fun at the sex whose rules she is about to subvert. Not for the only time in Shakespeare, we see a stage full of men who need a woman to sort out their problems.

Portia may also be seen as bringing fresh air from Belmont into the sea-level miasma of Venice, and readings of the play have often been constructed around a sharp opposition between the two locations, between the values of Portia and the values of Shylock. Shakespeare, however, will not leave it at that; there are constant echoes back and forth between the play's apparently disparate worlds. Portia gives a ring to Bassanio, who gives it away; Leah gave a ring to Shylock, and Jessica steals it. Keys lock Shylock's house and unlock the caskets of Belmont. Portia calls Bassanio "dear bought" (3.2.326) and Shylock uses almost the same words for his pound of flesh, which is "dearly bought" (4.1.101). Shylock's proverb, "Fast bind, fast find" (2.5.55), could be a comment on the way the women use the rings to bind the men to them. His claim on Antonio's body is grotesque, but the adultery jokes of the final scene remind us that married couples also claim exclusive rights in each other's bodies. Marriage is mutual ownership, and Shylock's recurring cry of "mine!" echoes throughout the play.

The final images of harmony are a bit precarious. The moonlight reminds Lorenzo and Jessica of stories of tragic, betrayed love, in which they teasingly include their own. These stories are stylized and distanced, but not just laughed off as the tale of Pyramus and Thisbe is in *A Midsummer Night's Dream*. The problem of the rings *is* laughed off, but there is some pain and anxiety behind the laughter. The stars are "patens of bright gold" (5.1.67)—that is, plates used in the Eucharist which are also rich material objects. The play's materialism touches even the spiritual realm, and Lorenzo's eloquent account of the music of the spheres ends with a reminder that "we cannot hear it" (5.1.73). When Portia describes the beauty of the night, she creates a paradox: "This night methinks is but the daylight sick; / It looks a little paler" (5.1.137–38). So, as we watch the lovers go off to bed, we may think of their happiness, or of the human cost to those who have been excluded; we may wonder how much it matters that this happiness was bought in part with Shylock's money. A brilliant night, or a sickly day? We may feel that this is another harmony whose music eludes us. Or we may conclude that the happiness is all the more precious for being hard-won, and all the more believable for the play's acknowledgment that love is part of the traffic of the world.

Further Reading

The Merchant of Venice

Auden, W. H. "Brothers and Others." In *The Dyer's Hand and Other Essays*, pp. 218–37. London: Faber & Faber, 1963.

Auden classes *The Merchant of Venice* among Shakespeare's "unpleasant plays" because the attraction we feel toward the "romantic fairy story of Belmont" is constantly undercut by the historical reality of "money-making Venice." The presence of Antonio and Shylock reminds us that the utopian qualities of Belmont are illusory.

Barton, John. "Exploring a Character: Playing Shylock." In *Playing Shakespeare*, pp. 169–80. London: Methuen, 1984.

This discussion between Barton and two actors he has directed as Shylock centers initially on the question of the play's anti-Semitism. After agreeing that the play resists anti-Semitism, the two actors outline their different approaches to individual scenes, finding that the key to the role is to "play the inconsistencies."

Ben-Sasson, H. H. *The History of the Jewish People*, pp. 385–723. Cambridge: Harvard University Press, 1976.

Ben-Sasson chronicles a thousand-year period of Jewish history, including the Middle Ages and the English Renaissance. Throughout this epoch, Jewish people lived under the rule of Christianity and Islam, monotheistic religions that, although they had developed out of the religious concepts of Judaism, claimed a truer conception of those tenets. Ben-Sasson therefore maintains that the persecution of Jews was an act of "deliberate policy."

Boose, Lynda. "The Comic Contract and Portia's Golden Ring." *Shakespeare Studies* 20 (1988): 241–54.
     Boose pursues the connection between the "comic contract"—that between play and audience—and the role of the comic heroine. The play is "transferred to the hands of its audience" in an exchange similar to the delivery of the bride to the groom by her father. In *The Merchant of Venice*, however, Portia threatens the contract by excluding all suitors "outside her own social, ethnic, religious, and linguistic group."

Bulman, J. C. *Shakespeare in Performance: The Merchant of Venice*. Manchester: Manchester University Press, 1991.
     With reference to selected stage and screen presentations, Bulman investigates how Shakespeare's text has been realized in production. The study includes discussion of how practical considerations influence the meaning of *The Merchant of Venice* onstage: the stage the actor plays on, the acting company, the players' abilities, as well as political, social, and economic conditions of performance.

Cohen, Derek. "Shylock and the Idea of the Jew." In *Shakespearean Motives*, pp. 104–18. New York: St. Martin's Press, 1988.
     Cohen unequivocally calls *The Merchant of Venice* a "crudely anti-Semitic play," then examines the paradox that follows from this assertion: the fact that while Shylock is the drama's villain, he is also its victim. Cohen concludes that the final scene reveals that Shakespeare knew Jews were human beings, but chose to exploit a cruel stereotype for "mercenary and artistic

reasons," a possibility Cohen finds "profoundly troubling."

Cooper, John R. "Shylock's Humanity." *Shakespeare Quarterly* 21 (1970): 117–24.

After surveying the critical debate over Shylock, Cooper argues that he is neither villainous nor sentimental but a character with a real if limited viewpoint. In Cooper's reading of Shylock's "I am a Jew" speech, Shakespeare is not inviting the audience to rebuke or ridicule Shylock but to empathize with what is a "universal issue."

Danson, Lawrence. *The Harmonies of The Merchant of Venice*. New Haven: Yale University Press, 1978.

Danson focuses on the circle as the play's most pervasive figure. He divides the play into three connected episodes, in each of which "an apparently insoluble dilemma is resolved as opposing ends join in a ring of harmony." Thus the play's contrasting pairs—law/freedom, justice/mercy, friendship/marriage, Jew/Christian, Venice/Belmont—"interlock into a concordant whole."

Jardine, Lisa. "Cultural Confusion and Shakespeare's Learned Heroine: 'These are old paradoxes.'" *Shakespeare Quarterly* 38 (1987): 1–18.

Jardine follows "the traces of the learned woman in . . . the texts of two of Shakespeare's plays," pursuing the ambivalence about a "woman's place" in Renaissance intellectual life. In *Merchant,* Portia's knowledge of the law elicits "two versions of a confused cultural response" to educated women: the woman as "powerfully chaste and loyal" in her capacity as a woman of "manly spirit/mind"; and the educated woman whose authority and knowledge elicit fear.

Lelyveld, Toby. *Shylock on the Stage*. Cleveland: The Press of Western Reserve University, 1960.

Tracing the manner in which Shylock has been characterized onstage from Shakespeare's day to the present, Lelyveld discusses the changing conception of Shylock as presented by actors such as Edmund Kean, Edwin Booth, and Henry Irving. The development, according to Lelyveld, has been from a character that confirmed the Elizabethan conception of the villainy of Jews to a figure that evokes profound sympathy from today's audience.

Lewalski, Barbara K. "Biblical Allusion and Allegory in *The Merchant of Venice*." *Shakespeare Quarterly* 13 (1962): 327–43.

Concentrating upon the allegorical organization of *Merchant*, Lewalski finds that allegorical significance is arranged generally on four levels: a "literal or story level"; a level concerned with truths relating to humanity and Christ; a level dealing with factors "in the moral development of the individual"; and a level treating "the ultimate reality, the Heavenly City."

Marlowe, Christopher. *The Jew of Malta* (c. 1589). In *Christopher Marlowe: The Complete Plays*, edited by J. B. Steane. Harmondsworth: Penguin, 1969.

Shylock's relationship with Jessica has obvious parallels with that of Marlowe's flamboyant villain-hero, Barabas, and his daughter, Abigail. Unlike Jessica, Abigail at first aids her father in his acts of revenge against the Christians. But later, like Jessica, Abigail flees her father (who has tricked her beloved into a fatal duel with a supposed rival) and becomes a Christian.

Midgley, Graham. "*The Merchant of Venice:* A Reconsideration." *Essays in Criticism* 10 (1960): 119–33.

Midgley argues that the two focal points of the play are Shylock and Antonio, and that the world of love and marriage is opposed by the social, political, and economic world of Venice. As Shylock is to Venetian society, so is Antonio to the world of love and marriage. For Midgley, Antonio and Shylock are both outsiders and therefore the play is a "twin study in loneliness."

Newman, Karen. "Portia's Ring: Unruly Women and Structures of Exchange in *The Merchant of Venice.*" *Shakespeare Quarterly* 38 (1987): 19–33.

The Merchant of Venice is a study in inversion for Newman, because in early modern England "a woman occupying the position of . . . lawyer in a Renaissance Venetian courtroom . . . is not the same as a man doing so." The play in these terms "resists the 'traffic in women,'" and "interrogates the Elizabethan sex/gender system."

Overton, Bill. *The Merchant of Venice: Text and Performance.* London: Macmillan, 1987.

Overton discusses the play's text in terms of its set of contrasts. Then, referring closely to five British stage and television productions between 1970 and 1984, he sketches out the ways in which these contradictions can be successfully, and unsuccessfully, staged. Overton favors productions that "break down" the barrier between audience and performer and therefore sharpen the focus on the play's contradictions in matters of gender and race.

Rabkin, Norman. "Meaning and *The Merchant of Venice.*" In *Shakespeare and the Problem of Meaning*, pp. 1–32. Chicago: University of Chicago Press, 1981.

Rabkin explores the tensions, contradictions, and mixed signals that the play generates. *The Merchant of*

Venice demands constant reassessment and "inconsistent responses" from an audience, and Rabkin therefore argues against interpretations that find "meaning as the principle of unity in a work."

Tennenhouse, Leonard. "The Counterfeit Order of *The Merchant of Venice*." In *Representing Shakespeare: New Psychoanalytic Essays*, edited by Murray M. Schwartz and Coppélia Kahn, pp. 54–69. Baltimore: Johns Hopkins University Press, 1980.

For Tennenhouse, Shakespeare's design of opposition in composing *The Merchant of Venice* signals a desire to create a dramatic world that was "whole, social, and stable." But the resolving of opposition in the play also signals "disturbance, conflict, and anxiety," for the opposition reflects psychological tensions.

Wilson, Thomas. *A Discourse upon Usury* (1572). Introduction by R. H. Tawney. London: G. Bell & Sons, 1925.

This account of usury, first published in 1572, is written in the form of a debate. Chapters include "The Needy Gentleman," "The Damnable Sin of Usury," and "The Harrying of the Usurer." Tawney's introduction places the subject of usury in its historical context.

Shakespeare's Language

Abbott, E. A. *A Shakespearian Grammar*. New York: Haskell House, 1972.

This compact reference book, first published in 1870, helps with many difficulties in Shakespeare's language. It systematically accounts for a host of differences between Shakespeare's usage and sentence structure, and our own.

Blake, Norman. *Shakespeare's Language: An Introduction.* New York: St. Martin's Press, 1983.
This general introduction to Elizabethan English discusses various aspects of the language of Shakespeare and his contemporaries, offering possible meanings for hundreds of ambiguous constructions.

Dobson, E. J. *English Pronunciation, 1500–1700.* 2 vols. Oxford: Clarendon Press, 1968.
This long and technical work includes chapters on spelling (and its reformation), phonetics, stressed vowels, and consonants in early modern English.

Houston, John. *Shakespearean Sentences: A Study in Style and Syntax.* Baton Rouge: Louisiana State University Press, 1988.
Houston studies Shakespeare's stylistic choices, considering matters such as sentence length and the relative positions of subject, verb, and direct object. Examining plays throughout the canon in a roughly chronological, developmental order, he analyzes how sentence structure is used in setting tone, in characterization, and for other dramatic purposes.

Onions, C. T. *A Shakespeare Glossary.* Oxford: Clarendon Press, 1986.
This revised edition updates Onions's standard, selective glossary of words and phrases in Shakespeare's plays that are now obsolete, archaic, or obscure.

Partridge, Eric. *Shakespeare's Bawdy.* London: Routledge & Kegan Paul, 1955.
After an introductory essay, "The Sexual, the Homosexual, and Non-Sexual Bawdy in Shakespeare," Partridge provides a comprehensive glossary of "bawdy" phrases and words from the plays.

Robinson, Randal. *Unlocking Shakespeare's Language: Help for the Teacher and Student*. Urbana, Ill.: National Council of Teachers of English and the ERIC Clearinghouse on Reading and Communication Skills, 1989.

Specifically designed for the high-school and undergraduate college teacher and student, Robinson's book addresses the problems that most often hinder present-day readers of Shakespeare. Through work with his own students, Robinson found that many readers today are particularly puzzled by such stylistic characteristics as subject-verb inversion, interrupted structures, and compression. He shows how our own colloquial language contains comparable structures, and thus helps students recognize such structures when they find them in Shakespeare's plays. This book supplies worksheets—with examples from major plays—to illuminate and remedy such problems as unusual sequences of words and the separation of related parts of sentences.

Shakespeare's Life

Baldwin, T. W. *William Shakspere's Petty School*. Urbana: University of Illinois Press, 1943.

Baldwin here investigates the theory and practice of the petty school, the first level of education in Elizabethan England. He focuses on that educational system primarily as it is reflected in Shakspere's art.

Baldwin, T. W. *William Shakspere's Small Latine and Lesse Greeke*. 2 vols. Urbana: University of Illinois Press, 1944.

Baldwin attacks the view that Shakespeare was an uneducated genius—a view that had been dominant among Shakespeareans since the eighteenth century. Instead, Baldwin shows, the educational system of

Shakespeare's time would have given the playwright a strong background in the classics, and there is much in the plays that shows how Shakespeare benefited from such an education.

Beier, A. L., and Roger Finlay, eds. *London 1500–1800: The Making of the Metropolis*. New York: Longman, 1986.
   Focusing on the economic and social history of early modern London, these collected essays probe aspects of metropolitan life, including "Population and Disease," "Commerce and Manufacture," and "Society and Change."

Bentley, G. E. *Shakespeare's Life: A Biographical Handbook*. New Haven: Yale University Press, 1961.
   This "just-the-facts" account presents the surviving documents of Shakespeare's life against an Elizabethan background.

Chambers, E. K. *William Shakespeare: A Study of Facts and Problems*. 2 vols. Oxford: Clarendon Press, 1930.
   Analyzing in great detail the scant historical data, Chambers's complex, scholarly study considers the nature of the texts in which Shakespeare's work is preserved.

Cressy, David. *Education in Tudor and Stuart England*. London: Edward Arnold, 1975.
   This volume collects sixteenth-, seventeenth-, and early-eighteenth-century documents detailing aspects of formal education in England, such as the curriculum, the control and organization of education, and the education of women.

Dutton, Richard. *William Shakespeare: A Literary Life*. New York: St. Martin's Press, 1989.

Not a biography in the traditional sense, Dutton's very readable work nevertheless "follows the contours of Shakespeare's life" as he examines Shakespeare's career as playwright and poet, with consideration of his patrons, theatrical associations, and audience.

Fraser, Russell. *Young Shakespeare*. New York: Columbia University Press, 1988.
Fraser focuses on Shakespeare's first thirty years, paying attention simultaneously to his life and art.

De Grazia, Margreta. *Shakespeare Verbatim: The Reproduction of Authenticity and the Apparatus of 1790*. Oxford: Clarendon Press, 1991.
De Grazia traces and discusses the development of such editorial criteria as authenticity, historical periodization, factual biography, chronological developments, and close reading, locating as the point of origin Edmond Malone's 1790 edition of Shakespeare's works. There are interesting chapters on the First Folio and on the "legendary" versus the "documented" Shakespeare.

Schoenbaum, S. *William Shakespeare: A Compact Documentary Life*. New York: Oxford University Press, 1977.
This standard biography economically presents the essential documents from Shakespeare's time in an accessible narrative account of the playwright's life.

Shakespeare's Theater

Bentley, G. E. *The Profession of Player in Shakespeare's Time, 1590–1642*. Princeton: Princeton University Press, 1984.
Bentley readably sets forth a wealth of evidence about performance in Shakespeare's time, with special atten-

tion to the relations between player and company, and the business of casting, managing, and touring.

Berry, Herbert. *Shakespeare's Playhouses*. New York: AMS Press, 1987.

Berry's six essays collected here discuss (with illustrations) varying aspects of the four playhouses in which Shakespeare had a financial stake: the Theatre in Shoreditch, the Blackfriars, and the first and second Globe.

Cook, Ann Jennalie. *The Privileged Playgoers of Shakespeare's London*. Princeton: Princeton University Press, 1981.

Cook's work argues, on the basis of sociological, economic, and documentary evidence, that Shakespeare's audience—and the audience for English Renaissance drama generally—consisted mainly of the "privileged."

Greg, W. W. *Dramatic Documents from the Elizabethan Playhouses*. 2 vols. Oxford: Clarendon Press, 1931.

Greg itemizes and briefly describes almost all the play manuscripts that survive from the period 1590 to around 1660, including, among other things, players' parts. His second volume offers facsimiles of selected manuscripts.

Gurr, Andrew. *Playgoing in Shakespeare's London*. Cambridge: Cambridge University Press, 1987.

Gurr charts how the theatrical enterprise developed from its modest beginnings in the late 1560s to become a thriving institution in the 1600s. He argues that there were important changes over the period 1567–1644 in the playhouses, the audience, and the plays.

Harbage, Alfred. *Shakespeare's Audience*. New York: Columbia University Press, 1941.

Harbage investigates the fragmentary surviving evidence to interpret the size, composition, and behavior of Shakespeare's audience.

Hattaway, Michael. *Elizabethan Popular Theatre: Plays in Performance*. London: Routledge & Kegan Paul, 1982.

Beginning with a study of the popular drama of the late Elizabethan age—a description of the stages, performance conditions, and acting of the period—this volume concludes with an analysis of five well-known plays of the 1590s, one of them (*Titus Andronicus*) by Shakespeare.

Shapiro, Michael. *Children of the Revels: The Boy Companies of Shakespeare's Time and Their Plays*. New York: Columbia University Press, 1977.

Shapiro chronicles the history of the amateur and quasi-professional child companies that flourished in London at the end of Elizabeth's reign and the beginning of James's.

The Publication of Shakespeare's Plays

Blayney, Peter. *The First Folio of Shakespeare*. Hanover, Md.: Folger, 1991.

Blayney's accessible account of the printing and later life of the First Folio—an amply illustrated catalogue to a 1991 Folger Shakespeare Library exhibition—analyzes the mechanical production of the First Folio, describing how the Folio was made, by whom and for whom, how much it cost, and its ups and downs (or, rather, downs and ups) since its printing in 1623.

Hinman, Charlton. *The Printing and Proof-Reading of the First Folio of Shakespeare.* 2 vols. Oxford: Clarendon Press, 1963.

In the most arduous study of a single book ever undertaken, Hinman attempts to reconstruct how the Shakespeare First Folio of 1623 was set into type and run off the press, sheet by sheet. He also provides almost all the known variations in readings from copy to copy.

Hinman, Charlton. *The Norton Facsimile: The First Folio of Shakespeare.* New York: W. W. Norton, 1968.

This facsimile presents a photographic reproduction of an "ideal" copy of the First Folio of Shakespeare; Hinman attempts to represent each page in its most fully corrected state.

Key to
Famous Lines and Phrases

In sooth I know not why I am so sad.
[Antonio—1.1.1]

I hold the world but as the world . . .
A stage where every man must play a part,
And mine a sad one.   [Antonio—1.1.81–83]

Let me play the fool.   [Gratiano—1.1.84]

"I am Sir Oracle,
And when I ope my lips, let no dog bark!"
[Gratiano—1.1.98–99]

Gratiano speaks an infinite deal of nothing. . . .
[Bassanio—1.1.121]

By my troth, Nerissa, my little body is aweary of this
great world.   [Portia—1.2.1–2]

It is a good divine that follows his own instructions.
[Portia—1.2.14–15]

God made him, and therefore let him pass for a man.
[Portia—1.2.56–57]

The devil can cite Scripture for his purpose!
[Antonio—1.3.107]

It is a wise father that knows his own child.
[Lancelet—2.2.74–75]

Truth will come to light . . . in the end, truth will out.
[Lancelet—2.2.77–79]

But love is blind, and lovers cannot see
The pretty follies that themselves commit. . . .
[Jessica—2.6.37–38]

All that glisters is not gold. . . .   [Scroll—2.7.73]

Now, what news on the Rialto?   [Solanio—3.1.1]

Hath not a Jew eyes?   [Shylock—3.1.57–58]

Tell me where is fancy bred. . . .   [Song—3.2.65]

Yes, truly, for look you, the sins of the father are to be
laid upon the children.   [Lancelet—3.5.1–2]

I am a tainted wether of the flock,
Meetest for death.   [Antonio—4.1.116–17]

I never knew so young a body with so old a head.
[Letter—4.1.164–65]

The quality of mercy is not strained. [Portia—4.1.190]

The moon shines bright. In such a night as this. . . .
[Lorenzo—5.1.1]

How sweet the moonlight sleeps upon this bank.
[Lorenzo—5.1.62]

I am never merry when I hear sweet music.
[Jessica—5.1.77]

The man that hath no music in himself . . .
Is fit for treasons, stratagems, and spoils. . . .
                              [Lorenzo—5.1.92–94]

How far that little candle throws his beams!
So shines a good deed in a naughty world.
                              [Portia—5.1.99–100]

. . . the moon sleeps with Endymion
And would not be awaked!   [Portia—5.1.118–19]

THE FOLGER
SHAKESPEARE LIBRARY

The world's leading center for Shakespeare studies presents
acclaimed editions of Shakespeare's plays.

All's Well That Ends Well

Antony and Cleopatra

As You Like It

The Comedy of Errors

Cymbeline

Hamlet

Henry IV, Part 1

Henry IV, Part 2

Henry V

Henry VI, Part 1

Henry VI, Part 2

Henry VI, Part 3

Henry VIII

Julius Caesar

King John

King Lear

Love's Labor's Lost

Macbeth

Measure for Measure

The Merchant of Venice

The Merry Wives of Windsor

A Midsummer Night's Dream

Much Ado About Nothing

Othello

Pericles

Richard II

Richard III

Romeo and Juliet

Shakespeare's Sonnets

Shakespeare's Sonnets
 and Poems

The Taming of the Shrew

The Tempest

Timon of Athens

Titus Andronicus

Troilus and Cressida

Twelfth Night

The Two Gentlemen of Verona

The Winter's Tale

Three Comedies: The Taming
 of the Shrew/A Midsummer
 Night's Dream/Twelfth Night

Three Tragedies: Hamlet/
 Macbeth/Romeo and Juliet

For more information on Folger Shakespeare Library Editions, including
Shakespeare Set Free teaching guides, visit www.simonsays.com.

**SIMON & SCHUSTER
PAPERBACKS**
A CBS COMPANY